Simple
Instant Pot®
RECIPES

Publications International, Ltd.

Instant Pot
CONTENTS

INTRODUCTION TO INSTANT POT®

Everyday cooking made quick and easy

Preparing one, two or three meals a day can be exhausting, so let your Instant Pot—and the magic of pressure cooking—do the work for you. The recipes in this book were designed to minimize the time and energy you spend on cooking, with shorter ingredient lists, fewer steps and less cooking time than conventional recipes. So hearty soups, spicy chilies, even savory stews can all become weeknight favorites.

Why use a pressure cooker?

Spped is the main reason. In pressure cooking, liquid is heated in a heavy pot with a lid that locks and forms an airtight seal. Since the steam from the hot liquid is trapped inside and can't evaporate, the pressure increases and raises the boiling point of the contents in the pot, and these items cook faster at a higher temperature. In general, pressure cooking can reduce cooking time to about one third of the time used in conventional cooking methods—and typically the time spent on pressure cooking is hands off. (There's no peeking or stirring when food is being cooked under pressure.)

What makes the Instant Pot different?

The Instant Pot is a versatile electric multi-cooker that can be a pressure cooker, rice cooker, slow cooker, steamer and yogurt maker. The cooking programs you'll find on the control panel are convenient shortcuts for some foods you may prepare regularly (rice, beans, etc.) which use preset times and cooking levels. But in these pages we'll explore the basics of pressure cooking with recipes that use the Pressure Cook or Manual button along with customized cooking times and pressure levels. These simple and delicious dishes will inspire you to use your Instant Pot daily and create your own Instant Pot magic!

Pancake Breakfast Casserole (page 24)

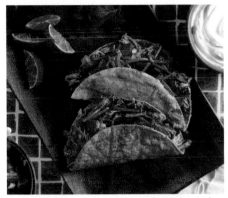

Tuesday Night Tacos (page 108)

Superfast Applesauce (page 180)

Instant Pot

Instant Pot Components

The **exterior pot** is where the electrical components are housed. It should never be immersed in water; to clean it, simply unplug the unit, wipe it with a damp cloth and dry it immediately.

The **inner pot** holds the food and fits snugly into the exterior pot. Made of stainless steel, it is removable, and it can be washed by hand or in the dishwasher.

The **LED display** shows a time that indicates where the pressure cooker is in a particular function. The time counts down to zero from the number of minutes that were programmed. (The timing begins once the machine reaches pressure.) For Keep Warm and Yogurt functions, the time counts up.

The **pressure release valve** is on top of the lid and is used to seal the pot or release steam. To seal the pot, move the valve to the Sealing position; to release pressure, move the valve to the Venting position. This valve can pop off to clean, and to make sure nothing is blocking it.

The **float valve** controls the amount of pressure inside the pressure cooker and indicates when pressure cooking is taking place. The valve rises once the contents of the pot reach working pressure; it drops down when all the pressure has been released after cooking.

The **anti-block shield** is a small stainless steel cage found on the inside of the lid that prevents the pressure cooker from clogging. It can be removed for cleaning.

The **silicone sealing ring** underneath the lid helps create a tight seal to facilitate pressure cooking. The sealing ring has a tendency to absorb strong odors from cooking (particularly from acidic ingredients); washing it regularly with warm soapy water or in the dishwasher will help these odors dissipate, as will storing your Instant Pot with the lid ring side up. If you cook both sweet and savory dishes frequently, you may want to purchase an extra sealing ring (so the scent of curry or pot roast doesn't affect your rice pudding or crème brûlée). Make sure to inspect the ring before cooking—if it has any splits or cracks, it will not work properly and should be replaced.

Instant Pot Cooking Basics

Every recipe is slightly different, but most include these basic steps. Read through the entire recipe before beginning to cook so you'll know what ingredients to add and when to add them, which pressure level to use, the cooking time and the release method.

1. **Sauté:** Many recipes call for sautéing vegetables or browning meat at the beginning of a recipe to add flavor. (Be sure to leave the lid off in this step.)

2. Add the ingredients as the recipe directs and secure the lid, making sure the arrow mark on the lid is aligned with the "close" mark and lock icon on the rim of the outside pot. Turn the pressure release valve to the Sealing position.

3. Select Pressure Cook or Manual, then choose the pressure level. The default setting is high pressure, which is what most recipes in this book use. To change to low pressure, use the Pressure Level or Adjust button. To set the cooking time, use the + and - buttons. The Instant Pot will start automatically.

4. Once the pressure cooking is complete, use the pressure release method directed by the recipe. There are three types of releases:

Natural release:

Let the pressure slowly release on its own, which can take anywhere from 5 to 25 minutes (but is typically in the 10- to 15-minute range). The release time will be shorter for a pot that is less full and longer for one that is more full. When the float valve lowers, the pressure is released and you can open the lid.

Quick release:

Use a towel or pot holder to manually turn the pressure valve to the Venting position immediately after the cooking is complete. (Be sure to get out of the way of the steam before turning the valve.) It can take up to 2 minutes to fully release all the pressure; the float valve will drop down when all the pressure is released.

A combination of natural and quick release:

The recipe will instruct you to let the pressure release naturally for a certain amount of time (frequently for 10 minutes), and then do a quick release as directed.

Tips, Tricks, Dos and Don'ts

- Read the manual before beginning. There may be features you won't use, but it will eliminate some beginner's confusion, and it can help you understand how the Instant Pot works—and see all its possibilities. Models also change over time, so the manual can provide the best information about the buttons and functions of your pot. (Note that the terms "Pressure Cook" and "Manual" are interchangeable.)

- Don't overfill the pot—the total amount of food and liquid should not exceed the maximum level marked on the inner pot. Generally it is best not to fill the pot more than two thirds full; when cooking foods that expand during cooking such as beans and grains, do not fill it more than half full.

- Make sure there is always some liquid in the pot before cooking because a minimum amount is required to come up to pressure (the amount differs between models). However, if the recipe contains a large quantity of vegetables or meats, you may be able to use a bit less since these ingredients will create their own liquid.

- Always check that the pressure release valve is in the right position before you start pressure cooking. The food simply won't get cooked if the valve is not in the Sealing position because there will not be enough pressure in the pot.

- Never try to force the lid open after cooking—if the lid won't open, that means the pressure has not fully released. (As a safety feature, the lid remains locked until the float valve drops down.)

- Save the thickeners for after the pressure cooking is done. Pressure cooker recipes often end up with a lot of flavorful liquid left in the pot when cooking is complete; flour or cornstarch mixtures can thicken these liquids into delicious sauces. Use the Sauté function while incorporating the thickeners into the cooking liquid, and then cook and stir until the desired consistency is reached.

- Keep in mind that cooking times in some recipes may vary. We've included pressure cooking time charts as a guide (pages 184–187), but these are approximate times, and numerous variables may cause your results to be different. For example, the freshness of dried beans affects their cooking time (older beans take longer to cook), as does what they are cooked with—hard water (water that is high in mineral content), acidic ingredients, sugar and salt levels can also affect cooking times. So be flexible and experiment with what works best for you—you can always check the doneness of your food and add more time.

- Set reasonable expectations, i.e., don't expect everything you cook in the Instant Pot to be ready in a few minutes. Even though it reduces many conventional cooking times dramatically, nothing is literally "instant"—it will always take time to get up to pressure, and then to release it. (These machines are fast but not magical!)

Instant Pot
EASY BREAKFAST

Kale and Roasted Pepper Frittata
Makes 6 servings

10 eggs
½ cup whole milk
1 teaspoon Greek seasoning
2 cups baby kale*
1 cup (4 ounces) crumbled feta cheese with sun-dried tomatoes and basil

¾ cup diced roasted red peppers
1½ cups water

Or substitute 2 cups baby arugula or baby spinach.

1 Spray 1½-quart (6- to 7-inch) soufflé dish with nonstick cooking spray. Beat eggs, milk and Greek seasoning in medium bowl until well blended. Stir in kale, cheese and roasted peppers. Pour into prepared soufflé dish; cover with foil.

2 Pour water into Instant Pot; place rack in pot. Place soufflé dish on rack.

3 Secure lid and move pressure release valve to Sealing position. Press Pressure Cook or Manual; cook at high pressure 30 minutes.

4 When cooking is complete, use natural release for 10 minutes, then release remaining pressure. Remove soufflé dish from pot. Uncover; let stand 5 minutes before serving.

French Toast Casserole

Makes 6 servings

1 loaf (14 to 16 ounces) day-old cinnamon swirl bread (see Tip)	¼ cup maple syrup, plus additional for serving
4 ounces cream cheese, cubed	⅛ teaspoon salt
1½ cups whole milk	1 cup water
4 eggs	

1 Spray 1½-quart (6- to 7-inch) soufflé dish with nonstick cooking spray. Cut bread into 1-inch pieces. (You should have 5 to 6 cups bread cubes.) Place one third of bread in prepared soufflé dish; top with half of cream cheese cubes. Repeat layers; top with remaining bread.

2 Beat milk, eggs, ¼ cup maple syrup and salt in medium bowl until well blended. Pour over bread and cream cheese; press gently into liquid. Cover dish with foil; let stand 30 minutes.

3 Pour water into Instant Pot; place rack in pot. Place soufflé dish on rack. Secure lid and move pressure release valve to Sealing position. Press Pressure Cook or Manual; cook at high pressure 35 minutes.

4 When cooking is complete, use natural release for 5 minutes, then release remaining pressure. Remove soufflé dish from pot. Uncover; let stand 5 minutes before serving. Cut into wedges; serve warm with additional maple syrup.

Tips

Day-old bread is drier than fresh bread and better able to absorb the custard mixture in casseroles and bread puddings. If you only have fresh bread, bake the bread cubes on a baking sheet in a 350°F oven about 7 minutes or until lightly toasted.

Lemon Blueberry Oatmeal

Makes 4 servings

2 tablespoons butter

1¼ cups steel-cut oats

3¾ cups water

½ teaspoon salt

2 lemons

4 tablespoons honey, divided

¾ cup fresh blueberries

½ cup chopped toasted almonds*

To toast almonds, cook in small skillet over medium heat about 5 minutes or until lightly browned and fragrant, stirring frequently.

1 Press Sauté; melt butter in Instant Pot. Add oats, cook about 6 minutes or until oats are browned and fragrant, stirring frequently. Stir in water and salt; mix well.

2 Secure lid and move pressure release valve to Sealing position. Press Pressure Cook or Manual; cook at high pressure 12 minutes.

3 Grate 4 teaspoons peel from lemons; squeeze 3 tablespoons juice.

4 When cooking is complete, use natural release for 10 minutes, then release remaining pressure. Stir oats until smooth. Add lemon juice, 2 teaspoons grated peel and 2 tablespoons honey; mix well.

5 Top each serving with blueberries, almonds and remaining lemon peel; drizzle with remaining honey.

Crustless Spinach Quiche

Makes 6 servings

6 eggs
¾ cup half-and-half
¾ teaspoon Italian seasoning
½ teaspoon salt
½ teaspoon black pepper

1 package (10 ounces) frozen chopped spinach, thawed and squeezed dry
1 cup (4 ounces) shredded Italian cheese blend
1½ cups water

1 Spray 7-inch metal cake pan with nonstick cooking spray. Beat eggs, half-and-half, Italian seasoning, salt and pepper in medium bowl until well blended. Stir in spinach and cheese; mix well. Pour into prepared pan; cover with foil.

2 Pour water into Instant Pot; place rack in pot. Place pan on rack.

3 Secure lid and move pressure release valve to Sealing position. Press Pressure Cook or Manual; cook at high pressure 28 minutes.

4 When cooking is complete, use natural release for 5 minutes, then release remaining pressure. Remove pan from pot. Uncover; let stand 5 minutes before serving.

Tip

To remove the quiche from the pan for serving, run a knife around the edge of the pan to loosen. Invert the quiche onto a plate; invert again onto a second plate. Cut into wedges to serve.

Sticky Cinnamon Monkey Bread

Makes 6 to 8 servings

⅓ cup sugar

1 tablespoon ground cinnamon

1 container (about 16 ounces) refrigerated jumbo biscuits (8 biscuits)

¼ cup (½ stick) butter, melted

1 cup water

1 Spray 6-cup bundt pan with nonstick cooking spray. Combine sugar and cinnamon in medium bowl; mix well. Sprinkle 1 tablespoon cinnamon-sugar over bottom of prepared pan.

2 Separate biscuits; cut each biscuit into quarters. Dip each biscuit piece in butter; roll in cinnamon-sugar to coat. Layer biscuit pieces in prepared pan; cover with foil.

3 Pour water into Instant Pot; place rack in pot. Place pan on rack. Secure lid and move pressure release valve to Sealing position. Press Pressure Cook or Manual; cook at high pressure 25 minutes.

4 When cooking is complete, use natural release for 10 minutes, then release remaining pressure. Remove pan from pot. Uncover; let stand 10 minutes. Invert bread onto plate; serve warm.

Fruity Whole Grain Cereal
Makes 4 to 6 servings

2¼ cups water
¼ cup steel-cut oats
¼ cup uncooked pearl barley
¼ cup uncooked brown rice
½ teaspoon salt
½ cup milk

⅓ cup golden raisins
¼ cup finely chopped dried dates
¼ cup chopped dried plums
2 tablespoons packed brown sugar
½ teaspoon ground cinnamon

1 Combine water, oats, barley, rice and salt in Instant Pot; mix well.

2 Secure lid and move pressure release valve to Sealing position. Press Pressure Cook or Manual; cook at high pressure 20 minutes.

3 When cooking is complete, use natural release for 10 minutes, then release remaining pressure.

4 Stir in milk, raisins, dates, dried plums, brown sugar and cinnamon; mix well. Serve hot. Refrigerate any leftover cereal in airtight container.

Tip
To reheat cereal, place one serving in microwavable bowl. Microwave on HIGH 30 seconds; stir. Add water or milk to reach desired consistency. Microwave just until hot.

Apple Cinnamon Breakfast Risotto

Makes 6 servings

- 4 tablespoons (½ stick) butter, divided
- 4 medium Granny Smith apples (about 1½ pounds), peeled and diced
- 1½ teaspoons ground cinnamon, divided
- 1½ cups uncooked arborio rice
- 1 teaspoon salt
- ¼ teaspoon ground allspice
- 4 cups apple juice
- 2 tablespoons packed dark brown sugar, plus additional for serving
- 1 teaspoon vanilla
- Milk, sliced almonds and dried cranberries (optional)

1 Press Sauté; melt 2 tablespoons butter in Instant Pot. Add apples and ½ teaspoon cinnamon; cook and stir about 5 minutes or until apples are softened. Transfer to small bowl; set aside.

2 Melt remaining 2 tablespoons butter in pot. Add rice, remaining 1 teaspoon cinnamon, salt and allspice; cook and stir 1 minute. Stir in apple juice, 2 tablespoons brown sugar and vanilla; mix well.

3 Secure lid and move pressure release valve to Sealing position. Press Pressure Cook or Manual; cook at high pressure 6 minutes.

4 When cooking is complete, use quick release. Press Sauté; add reserved apples to pot. Cook and stir 1 minute or until risotto reaches desired consistency. Serve with milk, almonds, cranberries and additional brown sugar, if desired.

Pancake Breakfast Casserole

Makes 6 servings

4 eggs
1 cup half-and-half
2 tablespoons sugar
¾ teaspoon ground cinnamon, plus additional for garnish

½ teaspoon vanilla
9 frozen buttermilk pancakes (4-inch diameter), cut in half
1 cup water
Maple syrup

1 Spray 1½-quart (6- to 7-inch) soufflé dish with nonstick cooking spray. Beat eggs, half-and-half, sugar, ¾ teaspoon cinnamon and vanilla in medium bowl until well blended.

2 Arrange 4 or 5 pancake halves standing up around side of prepared soufflé dish. Stack remaining pancake halves in soufflé dish, making layers as even as possible. Pour egg mixture over pancakes; press pancakes gently into liquid. Cover dish with foil; refrigerate overnight.

3 Remove soufflé dish from refrigerator at least 30 minutes before cooking. Pour water into Instant Pot; place rack in pot. Place soufflé dish on rack. Secure lid and move pressure release valve to Sealing position. Press Pressure Cook or Manual; cook at high pressure 30 minutes.

4 When cooking is complete, use natural release for 5 minutes, then release remaining pressure. Remove soufflé dish from pot. Uncover; sprinkle with additional cinnamon, if desired. Cut into wedges; serve warm with maple syrup.

Instant Pot
SPEEDY SOUPS

One-Pot Chinese Chicken Soup

Makes 4 servings

- 1 container (32 ounces) chicken broth
- ⅓ cup reduced-sodium soy sauce
- 1 pound boneless skinless chicken thighs

- 1 package (16 ounces) frozen stir-fry vegetables (do not thaw)
- 6 ounces uncooked Chinese egg noodles
- 1 to 3 tablespoons sriracha sauce

1 Combine broth and soy sauce in Instant Pot; mix well. Add chicken. Secure lid and move pressure release valve to Sealing position. Press Pressure Cook or Manual; cook at high pressure 8 minutes.

2 When cooking is complete, use quick release. Remove chicken to bowl; set aside 5 minutes or until cool enough to handle. Shred chicken into bite-size pieces.

3 Press Sauté; add vegetables and noodles to broth mixture in pot. Cook about 3 minutes or until noodles are tender. Stir in chicken and 1 tablespoon sriracha sauce; taste and add additional sauce for a spicier flavor.

Beef Fajita Soup

Makes 8 servings

1 pound beef stew meat, cut into 1-inch pieces

1 can (about 15 ounces) pinto beans, rinsed and drained

1 can (about 15 ounces) black beans, rinsed and drained

1 can (about 14 ounces) beef broth

1 can (about 10 ounces) diced tomatoes with green chiles

1 green bell pepper, cut into ½-inch slices

1 red bell pepper, cut into ½-inch slices

1 onion, cut into ¼-inch slices

2 teaspoons ground cumin

1 teaspoon seasoned salt

½ teaspoon black pepper

Optional toppings: sour cream, shredded Monterey Jack or Cheddar cheese, chopped olives

1 Combine beef, beans, broth, tomatoes, bell peppers, onion, cumin, seasoned salt and black pepper in Instant Pot; mix well.

2 Secure lid and move pressure release valve to Sealing position. Press Pressure Cook or Manual; cook at high pressure 25 minutes.

3 When cooking is complete, use natural release for 10 minutes, then release remaining pressure. Serve with desired toppings.

Split Pea Soup

Makes 4 to 6 servings

8 slices bacon, chopped
1 onion, chopped
2 carrots, chopped
1 stalk celery, chopped
1 clove garlic, minced
½ teaspoon dried thyme
1 container (32 ounces) chicken broth

2 cups water
1 package (16 ounces) dried split peas, rinsed and sorted
¾ teaspoon salt
½ teaspoon black pepper
1 bay leaf

1 Press Sauté; cook bacon in Instant Pot until crisp. Remove to paper towel-lined plate. Drain off all but 1 tablespoon drippings.

2 Add onion, carrots and celery to pot; cook and stir 5 minutes or until vegetables are softened. Add garlic and thyme; cook and stir 1 minute. Stir in broth and water, scraping up browned bits from bottom of pot. Add split peas, half of bacon, salt, pepper and bay leaf; mix well.

3 Secure lid and move pressure release valve to Sealing position. Press Pressure Cook or Manual; cook at high pressure 8 minutes.

4 When cooking is complete, use natural release for 10 minutes, then release remaining pressure. Stir soup; remove and discard bay leaf. Garnish with remaining bacon.

Note

The soup may seem thin immediately after cooking, but it will thicken upon standing. If prepared in advance and refrigerated, thin the soup with water when reheating until it reaches the desired consistency.

Pozole

Makes 6 servings (about 6 cups)

1 tablespoon olive oil

1 large onion, cut in half and cut into ¼-inch slices

2 teaspoons dried oregano

1 clove garlic, minced

½ teaspoon ground cumin

12 ounces boneless skinless chicken thighs, cut into 1-inch strips

2 cans (4 ounces each) chopped green chiles

3 cups chicken broth

¼ teaspoon salt

1 package (10 ounces) frozen corn

1 can (2¼ ounces) sliced black olives, drained

Chopped fresh cilantro (optional)

Lime wedges (optional)

1 Press Sauté; heat oil in Instant Pot. Add onion; cook and stir about 3 minutes or until softened. Add oregano, garlic and cumin; cook and stir 1 minute. Stir in chicken and chiles. Add broth and salt; mix well.

2 Secure lid and move pressure release valve to Sealing position. Press Pressure Cook or Manual; cook at high pressure 5 minutes.

3 When cooking is complete, use natural release for 10 minutes, then release remaining pressure.

4 Press Sauté; add corn and olives to soup. Cook and stir 3 minutes or until heated through. Garnish with cilantro; serve with lime wedges, if desired.

Lentil Rice Soup

Makes 4 to 6 servings

1 tablespoon olive oil	1/8 teaspoon black pepper
1 onion, finely chopped	6 cups vegetable broth
2 carrots, finely chopped	1 cup dried lentils, rinsed and sorted
2 stalks celery, finely chopped	1/4 cup uncooked rice, rinsed well
2 teaspoons minced garlic	1/4 cup chopped fresh parsley
1 teaspoon salt	Sour cream (optional)
1 teaspoon herbes de Provence	

1 Press Sauté; heat oil in Instant Pot. Add onion, carrots, celery and garlic; cook and stir 5 minutes or until vegetables are softened. Add salt, herbes de Provence and pepper; cook and stir 30 seconds. Stir in broth, lentils and rice; mix well.

2 Secure lid and move pressure release valve to Sealing position. Press Pressure Cook or Manual; cook at high pressure 10 minutes.

3 When cooking is complete, use natural release for 10 minutes, then release remaining pressure. Stir in parsley. Top with sour cream, if desired.

Pork and Cabbage Soup

Makes 6 servings

8 ounces pork loin, cut into ½-inch pieces

1 medium onion, chopped

2 slices bacon, finely chopped

1 can (about 28 ounces) whole tomatoes, undrained, coarsely chopped

1 teaspoon salt

1 bay leaf

¾ teaspoon dried marjoram

⅛ teaspoon black pepper

¼ medium cabbage, chopped, divided (about 5 cups)

2 medium carrots, cut into ½-inch slices

1 cup chicken broth

2 tablespoons chopped fresh parsley

1 Press Sauté; add pork, onion and bacon to Instant Pot. Cook and stir about 5 minutes or until pork is no longer pink and onion is softened. Add tomatoes with liquid, salt, bay leaf, marjoram and pepper; cook 2 minutes, scraping up browned bits from bottom of pot. Stir in half of cabbage, carrots and broth; mix well.

2 Secure lid and move pressure release valve to Sealing position. Press Pressure Cook or Manual; cook at high pressure 8 minutes.

3 When cooking is complete, use natural release for 10 minutes, then release remaining pressure. Remove and discard bay leaf.

4 Press Sauté; add remaining half of cabbage to pot. Cook about 3 minutes or until cabbage is wilted, stirring frequently. Stir in parsley.

Mushroom Barley Soup

Makes 6 to 8 servings

2 tablespoons olive oil
1 onion, chopped
2 carrots, chopped
2 stalks celery, chopped
3 cloves garlic, minced
1 teaspoon salt
½ teaspoon dried thyme

½ teaspoon black pepper
5 cups vegetable or chicken broth
1 package (16 ounces) sliced
   mushrooms
½ cup uncooked pearl barley
½ ounce dried porcini or shiitake
   mushrooms

1 Press Sauté; heat oil in Instant Pot. Add onion, carrots and celery; cook and stir 5 minutes or until vegetables are softened. Add garlic, salt, thyme and pepper; cook and stir 1 minute. Stir in broth, sliced mushrooms, barley and dried mushrooms; mix well.

2 Secure lid and move pressure release valve to Sealing position. Press Pressure Cook or Manual; cook at high pressure 22 minutes.

3 When cooking is complete, use natural release for 10 minutes, then release remaining pressure.

Coconut Curry Chicken Soup

Makes 4 servings

1 can (about 13 ounces) coconut milk, divided

1½ cups chicken broth

1 cup chopped onion

2 tablespoons curry powder

1 teaspoon salt

½ teaspoon ground ginger

⅛ teaspoon ground red pepper

1½ pounds boneless skinless chicken thighs

¼ cup chopped fresh cilantro or mint

2 cups cooked rice (optional)

Lime wedges (optional)

1 Shake or stir coconut milk until well blended. Combine half of coconut milk, broth, onion, curry powder, salt, ginger and red pepper in Instant Pot; mix well. Add chicken, pressing into liquid.

2 Secure lid and move pressure release valve to Sealing position. Press Pressure Cook or Manual; cook at high pressure 9 minutes.

3 When cooking is complete, use natural release for 10 minutes, then release remaining pressure. Remove chicken to plate; let stand until cool enough to handle.

4 Shred chicken into bite-size pieces. Press Sauté; add chicken to pot with remaining coconut milk and cilantro. Cook 3 minutes or until heated through, stirring occasionally. Spoon rice over each serving, if desired; serve with lime wedges.

Easy Corn Chowder

Makes 4 servings

6 slices bacon, chopped

1 medium onion, diced

1 red bell pepper, diced

1 stalk celery, sliced

1 package (16 ounces) frozen corn, thawed

3 small potatoes, peeled and cut into ½-inch pieces (about 2 cups)

½ teaspoon ground coriander

3 cups chicken broth

½ teaspoon salt

½ teaspoon black pepper

¼ teaspoon ground red pepper

½ cup whipping cream

1 Press Sauté; cook bacon in Instant Pot until crisp. Remove to paper towel-lined plate. Drain off all but 1 tablespoon drippings.

2 Add onion, bell pepper and celery to pot; cook and stir 3 minutes or until vegetables are softened. Add corn, potatoes and coriander; cook and stir 1 minute. Stir in broth, salt, black pepper and ground red pepper; mix well.

3 Secure lid and move pressure release valve to Sealing position. Press Pressure Cook or Manual; cook at high pressure 4 minutes.

4 When cooking is complete, use natural release for 10 minutes, then release remaining pressure.

5 Press Sauté; cook 2 to 3 minutes or until soup thickens, partially mashing potatoes. Stir in cream; cook until heated through. Top with bacon.

Instant Pot®
HEARTY BOWLS

Salsa Verde Chicken Stew

Makes 4 to 6 servings

2 cans (about 15 ounces each) black beans, rinsed and drained

1½ pounds boneless skinless chicken breasts, cut into 1-inch pieces

1 jar (16 ounces) salsa verde

1½ cups frozen corn

¾ cup chopped fresh cilantro

Diced avocado (optional)

1 Combine beans, chicken and salsa in Instant Pot; mix well.

2 Secure lid and move pressure release valve to Sealing position. Press Pressure Cook or Manual; cook at high pressure 4 minutes.

3 When cooking is complete, use quick release. Press Sauté; add corn to pot. Cook about 3 minutes or until heated through. Stir in cilantro; mix well. Garnish with avocado.

White Chicken Chili

Makes 6 servings

1 tablespoon vegetable oil	1 teaspoon dried oregano
1½ pounds boneless skinless chicken breasts	¼ teaspoon black pepper
2 medium onions, chopped	¼ teaspoon ground red pepper
1 can (4 ounces) diced mild green chiles	1½ cups chicken broth
1 tablespoon minced garlic	2 cans (about 15 ounces each) Great Northern beans, rinsed and drained
2 teaspoons ground cumin	¼ cup chopped fresh cilantro
1 teaspoon salt	

1 Press Sauté; heat oil in Instant Pot. Add chicken; cook about 6 minutes or until browned on both sides. Remove to plate. Add onions and chiles to pot; cook and stir 3 minutes. Add garlic, cumin, salt, oregano, black pepper and red pepper; cook and stir 1 minute. Add broth, scraping up browned bits from bottom of pot. Stir in beans; mix well. Return chicken to pot, pressing into liquid.

2 Secure lid and move pressure release valve to Sealing position. Press Pressure Cook or Manual; cook at high pressure 7 minutes.

3 When cooking is complete, use quick release. Remove chicken to clean plate; set aside until cool enough to handle.

4 Shred chicken into bite-size pieces; return to pot. Press Sauté; cook 2 to 3 minutes or until chili thickens slightly. Sprinkle with cilantro.

Quick Shrimp and Okra Stew

Makes 4 servings

1 teaspoon vegetable oil

½ cup finely chopped onion

8 ounces okra, ends trimmed, cut into ½-inch slices

1 can (about 14 ounces) whole tomatoes, undrained, chopped

1 teaspoon dried thyme

¾ teaspoon salt

8 ounces medium raw shrimp, peeled and deveined

¾ cup fresh corn or thawed frozen corn

½ teaspoon hot pepper sauce

1 Press Sauté; heat oil in Instant Pot. Add onion; cook and stir 3 minutes or until softened. Add okra; cook and stir 3 minutes. Add tomatoes with juice, thyme and salt; mix well.

2 Secure lid and move pressure release valve to Sealing position. Press Pressure Cook or Manual; cook at high pressure 4 minutes.

3 When cooking is complete, use quick release.

4 Press Sauté; add shrimp, corn and hot pepper sauce to pot. Cook 3 minutes or until shrimp are pink and opaque, stirring frequently.

Chicken Enchilada Chili

Makes 4 servings

1 can (about 14 ounces) diced tomatoes with green chiles

1 can (10 ounces) red enchilada sauce

½ teaspoon salt

¼ teaspoon ground cumin

⅛ teaspoon black pepper

1½ pounds boneless skinless chicken thighs, cut into 1-inch pieces

1 cup frozen or canned corn

1½ tablespoons cornmeal

2 tablespoons finely chopped fresh cilantro

½ cup (2 ounces) shredded pepper jack cheese

Sliced green onions

1 Combine tomatoes, enchilada sauce, salt, cumin and pepper in Instant Pot; mix well. Add chicken; stir to coat.

2 Secure lid and move pressure release valve to Sealing position. Press Pressure Cook or Manual; cook at high pressure 5 minutes.

3 When cooking is complete, use natural release for 10 minutes, then release remaining pressure.

4 Press Sauté; add corn and cornmeal to pot. Cook about 6 minutes or until chili thickens, stirring frequently. Stir in cilantro. Sprinkle each serving with 2 tablespoons cheese; garnish with green onions.

Sweet Potato and Black Bean Chili

Makes 6 servings

1 tablespoon olive oil

1 large onion, chopped

4 teaspoons chili powder

2 cloves garlic, minced

1 teaspoon salt

1 teaspoon chipotle chili powder

½ teaspoon ground cumin

2 cans (about 15 ounces each) black beans, rinsed and drained

1 large sweet potato, peeled and cut into ½-inch pieces

1 can (about 14 ounces) diced tomatoes

1 can (about 14 ounces) crushed tomatoes

1½ cups vegetable broth or water

Optional toppings: sour cream, sliced green onions, shredded Cheddar cheese and/or tortilla chips

1 Press Sauté; heat oil in Instant Pot. Add onion; cook and stir 3 minutes or until softened. Add chili powder, garlic, salt, chipotle chili powder and cumin; cook and stir 1 minute. Add beans, sweet potato, diced tomatoes, crushed tomatoes and broth; mix well.

2 Secure lid and move pressure release valve to Sealing position. Press Pressure Cook or Manual; cook at high pressure 4 minutes.

3 When cooking is complete, use quick release.

4 Press Sauté; cook and stir 3 to 5 minutes or until chili thickens slightly. Serve with desired toppings.

Curried Chicken and Winter Vegetable Stew

Makes 4 to 6 servings

1 tablespoon vegetable oil

1 medium onion, chopped

1 tablespoon curry powder

1 clove garlic, minced

1 pound boneless skinless chicken breasts, cut into ½-inch pieces

1 can (about 14 ounces) diced tomatoes

1 cup chicken broth

2 medium turnips, cut into 1-inch pieces

2 medium carrots, cut into 1-inch slices

½ cup raisins (optional)

¼ cup tomato paste

1 teaspoon salt

⅛ teaspoon ground red pepper

1 Press Sauté; adjust heat to low. Heat oil in Instant Pot. Add onion; cook and stir 3 minutes or until softened. Add curry powder and garlic; cook and stir 1 minute. Stir in chicken, tomatoes, broth, turnips, carrots, raisins, if desired, tomato paste, salt and red pepper; mix well.

2 Secure lid and move pressure release valve to Sealing position. Press Pressure Cook or Manual; cook at high pressure 5 minutes.

3 When cooking is complete, use natural release for 5 minutes, then release remaining pressure.

Serving Suggestion

Serve with couscous or brown rice.

Black and White Chili

Makes 4 servings

1 tablespoon vegetable oil

1 pound chicken tenders, cut into ¾-inch pieces

1 cup coarsely chopped onion

1 can (about 14 ounces) fire-roasted diced tomatoes

1 can (about 15 ounces) Great Northern beans, rinsed and drained

1 can (about 15 ounces) black beans, rinsed and drained

2 tablespoons chili seasoning mix

½ teaspoon salt

Hot pepper sauce (optional)

1 Press Sauté; heat oil in Instant Pot. Add chicken and onion; cook and stir 5 minutes or until chicken begins to brown. Stir in tomatoes; cook 1 minute, scraping up browned bits from bottom of pot. Stir in beans, chili seasoning mix and salt; mix well.

2 Secure lid and move pressure release valve to Sealing position. Press Pressure Cook or Manual; cook at high pressure 5 minutes.

3 When cooking is complete, use natural release for 10 minutes, then release remaining pressure. Serve with hot pepper sauce, if desired.

Instant Pot
SANDWICH EXPRESS

Speedy Meatball Subs
Makes 6 servings

1 jar (24 ounces) pasta sauce

1 pound frozen Italian-style meatballs

6 sub or hoagie rolls, split

12 slices provolone cheese

Chopped fresh parsley (optional)

1 Pour half of pasta sauce into Instant Pot. Place meatballs in single layer in sauce; top with remaining sauce.

2 Secure lid and move pressure release valve to Sealing position. Press Pressure Cook or Manual; cook at high pressure 11 minutes. Preheat oven to 400°F. Line baking sheet with foil.

3 When cooking is complete, use quick release. Place rolls, cut sides down, on prepared baking sheet. Bake 3 minutes or until lightly toasted.

4 Spoon sauce and meatballs onto bottom halves of rolls; top with cheese slices (two per sandwich). Bake about 3 minutes or until cheese melts. Sprinkle with parsley, if desired; top with top halves of rolls.

Italian Beef Sandwiches

Makes 4 servings

1 jar (16 ounces) sliced pepperoncini	½ cup beef broth
1 jar (16 ounces) giardiniera	1 tablespoon Italian seasoning
2 to 2½ pounds boneless beef chuck roast	4 French or sub rolls, split

1 Drain pepperoncini, reserving ½ cup liquid. Set aside ½ cup pepperoncini for sandwiches. Drain giardiniera, reserving ½ cup vegetables for sandwiches.

2 Combine beef, remaining pepperoncini and reserved ½ cup pepperoncini liquid, remaining giardiniera vegetables, broth and Italian seasoning in Instant Pot.

3 Secure lid and move pressure release valve to Sealing position. Press Pressure Cook or Manual; cook at high pressure 60 minutes.

4 When cooking is complete, use natural release for 15 minutes, then release remaining pressure. Remove beef to large bowl; let stand until cool enough to handle. Shred beef into bite-size pieces. Add ½ cup cooking liquid; toss to coat.

5 Fill rolls with beef, reserved pepperoncini and reserved giardiniera vegetables. Serve with warm cooking liquid for dipping.

Pulled Pork Sandwiches

Makes 6 to 8 servings

2 tablespoons coarse salt
2 tablespoons packed brown sugar
2 tablespoons paprika
1 teaspoon dry mustard
1 teaspoon black pepper
1 boneless pork shoulder roast
     (about 3 pounds), cut into
     3-inch pieces

1 cup ketchup
⅓ cup cider vinegar
6 to 8 large hamburger rolls
     or buns, split
¾ cup barbecue sauce

1 Combine salt, brown sugar, paprika, mustard and pepper in small bowl; mix well. Rub mixture all over pork.

2 Combine ketchup and vinegar in Instant Pot; mix well. Place pork pieces in sauce; do not stir.

3 Secure lid and move pressure release valve to sealing position. Press Pressure Cook or Manual; cook at high pressure 60 minutes.

4 When cooking is complete, use natural release for 10 minutes, then release remaining pressure. Remove pork to large bowl; let stand until cool enough to handle.

5 Shred pork into bite-size pieces. Add ½ cup cooking liquid, if desired; toss to coat. Serve pork warm on rolls with barbecue sauce.

Hoisin Barbecue Chicken Sliders

Makes 16 sliders

2/3 cup hoisin sauce

1/3 cup barbecue sauce

1 tablespoon soy sauce

1/4 teaspoon red pepper flakes

3 to 3½ pounds boneless skinless chicken thighs

2 tablespoons water

1 tablespoon cornstarch

16 dinner rolls or Hawaiian sweet rolls, split

½ medium red onion, finely chopped

Sliced pickles (optional)

1 Combine hoisin sauce, barbecue sauce, soy sauce and red pepper flakes in Instant Pot; mix well. Add chicken; stir to coat.

2 Secure lid and move pressure release valve to Sealing position. Press Pressure Cook or Manual; cook at high pressure 8 minutes.

3 When cooking is complete, use natural release for 5 minutes, then release remaining pressure. Remove chicken to large plate; let stand until cool enough to handle. Shred chicken into bite-size pieces.

4 Stir water into cornstarch in small bowl until smooth. Press Sauté; add cornstarch mixture to pot. Cook and stir about 2 minutes or until sauce thickens. Return chicken to pot; mix well.

5 Spoon about ¼ cup chicken onto each roll; serve with onion and pickles, if desired.

Simple Sloppy Joes

Makes 6 servings

1½ pounds ground beef	1 tablespoon Worcestershire sauce
1 red bell pepper, chopped	1 tablespoon packed brown sugar
½ cup chopped onion	1 teaspoon chili powder
1 clove garlic, minced	1 can (about 8 ounces) baked beans
¼ cup ketchup	6 sandwich rolls, split
¼ cup barbecue sauce	¾ cup (3 ounces) shredded Cheddar cheese (optional)
2 tablespoons cider vinegar	

1 Press Sauté; add beef to Instant Pot. Cook about 8 minutes or until browned, stirring frequently. Drain off fat and excess liquid. Add bell pepper, onion and garlic to pot; cook and stir 3 minutes. Add ketchup, barbecue sauce, vinegar, Worcestershire sauce, brown sugar and chili powder; mix well.

2 Secure lid and move pressure release valve to Sealing position. Press Pressure Cook or Manual; cook at high pressure 10 minutes.

3 When cooking is complete, use quick release. Press Sauté; add beans to pot. Cook 5 minutes or until beef mixture thickens, stirring frequently.

4 Serve beef mixture on rolls; sprinkle with cheese, if desired.

Barbecue Beef Sandwiches

Makes 4 servings

2½ pounds boneless beef chuck roast, cut in half

2 tablespoons Southwest seasoning

1 tablespoon vegetable oil

½ cup beef broth

1½ cups barbecue sauce, divided

4 sandwich or pretzel buns, split

1⅓ cups prepared coleslaw* (preferably vinegar based)

*Prepared coleslaw can be found in the deli department at most supermarkets. Vinegar-based coleslaws provide a perfect complement to the rich beef; they can often be found at the salad bar or prepared foods section of large supermarkets.

1 Sprinkle both sides of beef with Southwest seasoning. Press Sauté; heat oil in Instant Pot. Add beef; cook about 6 minutes per side or until browned. Remove to plate.

2 Add broth to pot; cook 2 minutes, scraping up browned bits from bottom of pot. Stir in ½ cup barbecue sauce. Return beef to pot; turn to coat.

3 Secure lid and move pressure release valve to Sealing position. Press Pressure Cook or Manual; cook at high pressure 60 minutes.

4 When cooking is complete, use natural release for 15 minutes, then release remaining pressure. Remove beef to large bowl; let stand until cool enough to handle. Shred beef into bite-size pieces. Stir in remaining 1 cup barbecue sauce.

5 Fill buns with beef mixture; top with coleslaw.

Hot and Sweet Sausage Sandwiches

Makes 5 servings

1½ cups pasta sauce

1 large sweet onion, cut into ¼-inch slices

1 medium green bell pepper, cut into ½-inch slices

1 medium red bell pepper, cut into ½-inch slices

1½ tablespoons packed dark brown sugar

1 package (16 ounces) hot Italian sausage links (5 sausages)

5 Italian rolls, split

1 Combine pasta sauce, onion, bell peppers and brown sugar in Instant Pot; mix well. Add sausages to pot; spoon some of sauce mixture over sausages.

2 Secure lid and move pressure release valve to Sealing position. Press Pressure Cook or Manual; cook at high pressure 5 minutes.

3 When cooking is complete, use natural release for 10 minutes, then release remaining pressure. Remove sausages to plate; tent with foil.

4 Press Sauté; cook 10 minutes or until sauce is reduced by one third, stirring occasionally. Serve sausages in rolls; top with sauce.

Tip

If you have leftover sauce, refrigerate or freeze it and serve over pasta or polenta. Top with grated Parmesan cheese.

Chipotle BBQ Turkey Sandwiches

Makes 4 servings

1 tablespoon vegetable oil

1 small red onion, chopped

½ teaspoon chipotle chili powder

¾ cup plus 2 tablespoons barbecue sauce, divided

1 package (24 ounces) turkey tenderloins (2 tenderloins), each cut in half

4 sandwich buns

1 Press Sauté; heat oil in Instant Pot. Add onion; cook and stir 3 minutes or until softened. Add chili powder; cook and stir 30 seconds. Stir in ¾ cup barbecue sauce; mix well. Add turkey; turn to coat.

2 Secure lid and move pressure release valve to Sealing position. Press Pressure Cook or Manual; cook at high pressure 20 minutes.

3 When cooking is complete, use natural release for 10 minutes, then release remaining pressure. Remove turkey to large bowl; let stand 5 minutes. Shred turkey into bite-size pieces.

4 Meanwhile, press Sauté; adjust heat to low. Cook sauce in pot 5 minutes or until slightly reduced. Add shredded turkey and remaining 2 tablespoons barbecue sauce to pot; cook 2 minutes, stirring frequently. Serve on buns.

Quick French Dip

Makes 6 servings

3 pounds boneless beef chuck roast

½ teaspoon salt

½ teaspoon black pepper

1 tablespoon olive oil

2 onions, cut in half and cut into ¼-inch slices

⅔ cup reduced-sodium beef broth

3 tablespoons Worcestershire sauce

6 hoagie rolls, split

12 slices provolone cheese

1 Season beef with salt and pepper. Press Sauté; heat oil in Instant Pot. Add beef; cook about 6 minutes per side or until well browned. Remove to cutting board.

2 Add onions to pot; cook 8 minutes or until golden brown, stirring occasionally. Remove half of onions to small bowl; set aside. Add broth and Worcestershire sauce to pot; mix well. Cut beef into 3-inch pieces; add to pot and turn to coat.

3 Secure lid and move pressure release valve to Sealing position. Press Pressure Cook or Manual; cook at high pressure 45 minutes.

4 When cooking is complete, use natural release for 15 minutes, then release remaining pressure. Remove beef to large bowl; let stand until cool enough to handle. Shred beef into bite-size pieces. Add ⅔ cup cooking liquid; toss to coat. Strain remaining cooking liquid for serving, if desired. Preheat broiler. Line baking sheet with foil.

5 Place rolls cut sides up on prepared baking sheet; broil until lightly browned. Top bottom halves of rolls with cheese, beef and reserved onions. Serve with warm au jus for dipping.

Instant Pot®
ONE-POT PASTA

Snappy Spaghetti and Meatballs
Makes 6 servings

1 pound frozen meatballs

8 ounces uncooked spaghetti, broken in half

1 tablespoon olive oil

¾ teaspoon salt

2 cups water

1 jar (24 ounces) chunky marinara sauce

Grated Parmesan cheese and fresh basil leaves (optional)

1 Place meatballs in Instant Pot in single layer. Arrange pasta in criss-crossing layers over meatballs; drizzle with oil.

2 Stir salt into water in measuring cup. Pour marinara sauce and water over pasta, making sure to cover pasta completely. (Do not stir.)

3 Secure lid and move pressure release valve to Sealing position. Press Pressure Cook or Manual; cook at high pressure 9 minutes.

4 When cooking is complete, use quick release. Gently stir with tongs to separate pasta and blend with sauce. Garnish with cheese and basil.

Penne with Chunky Tomato Sauce and Spinach

Makes 4 servings

1 tablespoon olive oil
1 cup chopped onion
2 cloves garlic, minced
2 teaspoons salt
½ teaspoon dried oregano
½ teaspoon dried basil
¼ teaspoon red pepper flakes
¼ teaspoon black pepper

1 can (6 ounces) tomato paste
2 cups water
8 ounces uncooked penne pasta
1 package (5 ounces) baby spinach
1 large ripe tomato, seeded and chopped
¼ cup grated Parmesan cheese
¼ cup chopped fresh basil

1 Press Sauté; heat oil in Instant Pot. Add onion and garlic; cook and stir 3 minutes or until onion is softened. Add salt, oregano, dried basil, red pepper flakes and black pepper; cook and stir 30 seconds. Add tomato paste; cook and stir 1 minute. Add water; stir until well blended. Stir in pasta; mix well.

2 Secure lid and move pressure release valve to Sealing position. Press Pressure Cook or Manual; cook at high pressure 4 minutes.

3 When cooking is complete, use quick release. Stir in spinach and tomato; cover and let stand 2 to 3 minutes or until spinach is wilted. Top with cheese and fresh basil.

All-American Macaroni and Cheese

Makes 4 to 6 servings

2 cups uncooked elbow macaroni

2 cups water

1½ teaspoons salt, divided

1 can (5 ounces) evaporated milk

3 cups (12 ounces) shredded Colby-Jack cheese*

⅛ teaspoon black pepper

Or substitute 6 ounces each shredded Colby and Monterey Jack cheeses.

1 Combine macaroni, water and 1 teaspoon salt in Instant Pot. Secure lid and move pressure release valve to Sealing position. Press Pressure Cook or Manual; cook at high pressure 4 minutes.

2 When cooking is complete, use quick release.

3 Press Sauté; alternately add milk and handfuls of cheese, stirring constantly until cheese is melted and smooth. Stir in remaining ½ teaspoon salt and pepper.

Asian Chicken and Noodles

Makes 4 servings

1 tablespoon vegetable oil

1 pound boneless skinless chicken breasts, cut into 1×½-inch pieces

1 bottle or jar (about 12 ounces) stir-fry sauce

¾ cup chicken broth or water

8 ounces uncooked thin Pad Thai rice noodles (⅛ inch wide)

1 package (16 ounces) frozen stir-fry vegetable blend (do not thaw)

1 Press Sauté; heat oil in Instant Pot. Add chicken; cook about 4 minutes or until no longer pink, stirring frequently.

2 Stir in stir-fry sauce and broth; mix well. Top with noodles, breaking to fit as necessary. Cover with vegetables in even layer. (Do not stir.)

3 Secure lid and move pressure release valve to Sealing position. Press Pressure Cook or Manual; cook at high pressure 2 minutes.

4 When cooking is complete, use quick release. Stir with tongs to separate noodles and coat noodles and vegetables with sauce. If there is excess liquid in pot, press Sauté; cook and stir 2 minutes or until liquid has evaporated.

One-Pot Pasta with Sausage

Makes 6 servings

1 tablespoon olive oil

1 pound smoked sausage (about 4 links), cut into ¼-inch slices

1 onion, diced

1 tablespoon tomato paste

2 cloves garlic, minced

1½ teaspoons dried oregano

¼ teaspoon red pepper flakes

1 can (28 ounces) whole tomatoes, undrained, crushed with hands or coarsely chopped

2½ cups water

1½ teaspoons salt

1 package (16 ounces) uncooked cellentani pasta

1½ cups frozen peas

½ cup shredded Parmesan cheese

⅓ cup shredded fresh basil, plus additional for garnish

1 Press Sauté; heat oil in Instant Pot. Add sausage; cook about 7 minutes or until browned, stirring occasionally. Add onion; cook and stir 3 minutes or until softened. Add tomato paste, garlic, oregano and red pepper flakes; cook and stir 1 minute. Add tomatoes with liquid, water and salt; cook 2 minutes, scraping up browned bits from bottom of pot. Stir in pasta; mix well.

2 Secure lid and move pressure release valve to Sealing position. Press Pressure Cook or Manual; cook at high pressure 5 minutes.

3 When cooking is complete, use quick release.

4 Press Sauté; add peas to pot. Cook and stir 2 minutes. Turn off heat; stir in cheese and ⅓ cup basil. Cover and let stand 2 minutes. Garnish with additional basil.

Variation

You can substitute 1 pound uncooked Italian sausage (about 4 links) for the smoked sausage. Remove the casings, cut into ½-inch pieces and proceed with the recipe as directed.

Penne with Ricotta, Tomatoes and Basil

Makes 4 servings

2 cans (about 14 ounces each) diced tomatoes with basil, garlic and oregano

2½ cups water

3 teaspoons salt, divided

1 package (16 ounces) uncooked penne pasta

1 container (15 ounces) ricotta cheese

⅔ cup chopped fresh basil

¼ cup extra virgin olive oil

1 tablespoon balsamic vinegar

1 clove garlic, minced

¼ teaspoon black pepper

Grated Parmesan cheese

1 Combine tomatoes, water and 2 teaspoons salt in Instant Pot; mix well. Stir in pasta.

2 Secure lid and move pressure release valve to Sealing position. Press Pressure Cook or Manual; cook at high pressure 5 minutes.

3 Meanwhile, combine ricotta, basil, oil, vinegar, garlic, remaining 1 teaspoon salt and pepper in medium bowl; mix well.

4 When cooking is complete, use quick release. Drain any remaining liquid in pot. Add ricotta mixture to pot; stir gently to coat. Sprinkle with Parmesan just before serving.

Chili Spaghetti Supper

Makes 4 to 6 servings

1 pound lean ground beef	2 teaspoons chili powder
1 medium onion, chopped	¼ teaspoon garlic powder
1 teaspoon salt	8 ounces uncooked spaghetti
¼ teaspoon black pepper	½ cup water
1 can (about 15 ounces) chili beans in mild sauce	1½ cups (6 ounces) shredded sharp Cheddar cheese, divided
1 can (about 14 ounces) Italian-seasoned diced tomatoes	¼ cup sour cream

1 Press Sauté; add beef, onion, salt and pepper to Instant Pot. Cook about 8 minutes or until beef is no longer pink, stirring to break up meat. Drain fat.

2 Stir in beans, tomatoes, chili powder and garlic powder; mix well. Break spaghetti in half; add to pot with water.

3 Secure lid and move pressure release valve to Sealing position. Press Pressure Cook or Manual; cook at high pressure 5 minutes.

4 When cooking is complete, use quick release.

5 Press Sauté; stir in 1 cup cheese and sour cream. Cook and stir 1 minute or until cheese is melted and mixture is well blended. Turn off heat; cover and let stand 3 minutes or until excess liquid is absorbed and pasta is tender. Sprinkle with remaining ½ cup cheese.

Southwestern Mac and Cheese

Makes 6 to 8 servings

4 tablespoons (½ stick) butter, divided

1 onion, finely chopped

3⅓ cups water

1 package (16 ounces) uncooked elbow macaroni

1 can (about 14 ounces) diced tomatoes with green peppers and onions

1 teaspoon salt

4 cups (16 ounces) shredded Mexican cheese blend, divided

½ cup milk

1 cup salsa

1 Press Sauté; melt 1 tablespoon butter in Instant Pot. Add onion; cook and stir 3 minutes or until softened. Stir in water, macaroni, tomatoes and salt; mix well.

2 Secure lid and move pressure release valve to Sealing position. Press Pressure Cook or Manual; cook at high pressure 4 minutes.

3 When cooking is complete, use quick release.

4 Press Sauté; add 3½ cups cheese, milk and remaining 3 tablespoons butter to pot. Stir until smooth and well blended. Stir in salsa. Turn off heat. Sprinkle remaining ½ cup cheese over pasta; cover and let stand until melted.

Spicy Sausage and Penne Pasta
Makes 4 to 6 servings

- 1 pound uncooked bulk hot Italian sausage
- 1 cup chopped onion
- 2 cloves garlic, minced
- 2 teaspoons salt
- 1 teaspoon dried oregano
- 1 teaspoon dried basil
- 2 cans (about 14 ounces each) diced tomatoes
- 1½ cups water
- 8 ounces uncooked penne pasta
- 3 cups broccoli florets (from 1 medium head)
- ½ cup shredded Asiago or Romano cheese

1 Press Sauté; crumble sausage into Instant Pot. Add onion; cook 10 minutes or until sausage is cooked through, stirring frequently. Add garlic, salt, oregano and basil; cook and stir 1 minute. Stir in tomatoes, water and pasta; mix well.

2 Secure lid and move pressure release valve to Sealing position. Press Pressure Cook or Manual; cook at high pressure 3 minutes.

3 When cooking is complete, use quick release. Stir in broccoli. Secure lid and move pressure release valve to Sealing position. Press Pressure Cook or Manual; cook at high pressure 0 minutes. (Set cooking time for 0 minutes; pot will beep as soon as contents reach pressure.)

4 When cooking is complete, use quick release. Stir pasta; sprinkle with cheese.

Instant Pot
INSTANT DINNER

Perfect BBQ Ribs

Makes 4 servings

- 1 rack pork baby back ribs (about 3 pounds)
- ⅓ cup barbecue seasoning or grilling rub
- 2 cups apple juice
- ¼ cup cider vinegar
- 1 tablespoon liquid smoke
- 1 cup barbecue sauce, plus additional for serving

1 Remove membrane covering bones on underside of ribs. Rub barbecue seasoning generously over both sides of ribs, pressing to adhere.

2 Combine apple juice, vinegar and liquid smoke in Instant Pot; mix well. Stand ribs vertically in liquid, coiling ribs into a ring to fit in pot.

3 Secure lid and move pressure release valve to Sealing position. Press Pressure Cook or Manual; cook at high pressure 20 minutes. Preheat broiler. Line baking sheet with foil.

4 When cooking is complete, use natural release for 5 minutes, then release remaining pressure. Remove ribs to prepared baking sheet, meaty side up. Brush both sides of ribs with 1 cup barbecue sauce.

5 Broil about 5 minutes or until sauce begins to bubble and char. Cut into individual ribs; serve with additional sauce.

Rotisserie-Style Chicken

Makes 4 servings

- 1 whole chicken (about 4 pounds)
- 2 tablespoons rotisserie chicken seasoning (see Tip)
- 1 tablespoon butter
- 1 tablespoon olive oil
- 1 cup chicken broth
- Fresh parsley sprigs and lemon wedges (optional)

1 Pat chicken dry. Tie drumsticks together with kitchen string and tuck wing tips under. Sprinkle seasoning inside cavity and over all sides of chicken, pressing to adhere.

2 Press Sauté; heat butter and oil in Instant Pot. Add chicken, breast side up; cook about 5 minutes or until browned. Turn chicken over using tongs and spatula; cook about 5 minutes or until browned. Remove chicken to plate.

3 Add broth to pot; cook 1 minute, scraping up browned bits from bottom of pot. Place rack in pot; place chicken on rack, breast side up.

4 Secure lid and move pressure release valve to Sealing position. Press Pressure Cook or Manual; cook at high pressure 21 minutes.

5 When cooking is complete, use natural release for 15 minutes, then release remaining pressure. Remove chicken to cutting board; tent with foil and let stand 10 minutes before carving. If desired, strain cooking liquid and serve with chicken. Garnish with parsley and lemon wedges.

Tip

Rotisserie chicken seasoning is available in the spice section of many supermarkets. If unavailable, you can use a basic poultry seasoning or Italian seasoning combined with 1 teaspoon salt and 1 teaspoon paprika. Or use your favorite seasoning blend.

Note

When fully cooked, the temperature of the chicken (tested in the thigh) should be 165°F. A chicken larger than 4 pounds may take an additional 3 minutes to cook, while a smaller chicken will take a few minutes less.

Italian Beef Ragu

Makes 6 servings

2 pounds boneless beef chuck roast, cut into 2-inch pieces

½ teaspoon salt

½ teaspoon black pepper

1 tablespoon olive oil

1 onion, chopped

½ cup plus 2 tablespoons beef broth, divided

1 jar (24 ounces) garlic and herb pasta sauce

¼ cup plus 1 tablespoon red wine vinegar, divided

Hot cooked pappardelle pasta

Slivered fresh basil (optional)

Grated Parmesan cheese (optional)

1 Season beef with ½ teaspoon salt and ½ teaspoon pepper. Press Sauté; heat oil in Instant Pot. Add beef in two batches; cook about 5 minutes or until browned. Remove to plate. Add onion and 2 tablespoons broth to pot; cook 3 minutes or until softened, scraping up browned bits from bottom of pot. Reserve ¾ cup pasta sauce; set aside. Add remaining pasta sauce, ½ cup broth and ¼ cup vinegar to pot; mix well. Return beef and accumulated juices to pot; stir to coat.

2 Secure lid and move pressure release valve to Sealing position. Press Pressure Cook or Manual; cook at high pressure 45 minutes.

3 When cooking is complete, use natural release 15 minutes, then release remaining pressure. Remove beef to large bowl; let stand 5 minutes or until cool enough to handle.

4 Meanwhile, press Sauté; adjust heat to low. Add reserved ¾ cup pasta sauce and remaining 1 tablespoon vinegar to pot; cook 5 minutes, stirring occasionally.

5 Shred beef into bite-size pieces; stir into sauce. Taste and season with additional salt and pepper. Serve over pasta; garnish with basil and cheese.

Pork Picadillo

Makes 4 servings

1 tablespoon olive oil

1 pound boneless pork country-style ribs, trimmed and cut into ½-inch pieces

1 onion, chopped

2 cloves garlic, minced

1 can (about 14 ounces) diced tomatoes

½ cup raisins

2 tablespoons cider vinegar

2 canned chipotle peppers in adobo sauce, chopped

½ teaspoon salt

½ teaspoon ground cumin

½ teaspoon ground cinnamon

1 Press Sauté; heat oil in Instant Pot. Add pork; cook about 6 minutes or until browned, stirring occasionally. Add onion; cook and stir 2 minutes. Add garlic; cook and stir 30 seconds. Stir in tomatoes, raisins, vinegar, chipotle peppers, salt, cumin and cinnamon, scraping up browned bits from bottom of pot.

2 Secure lid and move pressure release valve to Sealing position. Press Pressure Cook or Manual; cook at high pressure 25 minutes.

3 When cooking is complete, use natural release for 10 minutes, then release remaining pressure. Stir pork mixture with tongs, breaking up pork into smaller pieces.

Quick Chicken Adobo

Makes 4 servings

⅓ cup cider vinegar
⅓ cup reduced-sodium soy sauce
5 cloves garlic, minced
3 bay leaves
1 teaspoon black pepper

2½ pounds bone-in skin-on chicken thighs (about 6)
Hot cooked rice (optional)
Sliced green onion (optional)

1 Combine vinegar, soy sauce, garlic, bay leaves and pepper in Instant Pot; mix well. Add chicken; turn to coat. Arrange chicken skin side down in liquid.

2 Secure lid and move pressure release valve to Sealing position. Press Pressure Cook or Manual; cook at high pressure 13 minutes. Preheat broiler. Line baking sheet with foil.

3 When cooking is complete, use natural release for 10 minutes, then release remaining pressure. Remove chicken to prepared baking sheet, skin side up.

4 Broil about 4 minutes or until skin is browned and crisp. Meanwhile, press Sauté; cook liquid in pot about 5 minutes or until slightly reduced. Serve sauce over chicken and rice, if desired. Garnish with green onion.

Chorizo Burritos

Makes 4 servings

12 ounces uncooked Mexican chorizo sausages, cut into bite-size pieces

2 green or red bell peppers, cut into 1-inch pieces

1 can (about 15 ounces) red beans, rinsed and drained

1 can (about 14 ounces) diced tomatoes

1 can (11 ounces) corn, drained

½ teaspoon ground cumin

½ teaspoon ground cinnamon

8 (8-inch) flour tortillas, warmed

2 cups hot cooked rice

1 cup (4 ounces) shredded Monterey Jack cheese

1 Combine chorizo, bell peppers, beans, tomatoes, corn, cumin and cinnamon in Instant Pot; mix well.

2 Secure lid and move pressure release valve to Sealing position. Press Pressure Cook or Manual; cook at high pressure 10 minutes.

3 When cooking is complete, use natural release for 10 minutes, then release remaining pressure.

4 Press Sauté; cook about 5 minutes or until chorizo mixture thickens, stirring occasionally.

5 Spoon chorizo mixture down centers of tortillas; top with rice and cheese. Roll up tortillas; serve immediately.

Miso Salmon

Makes 6 servings

½ cup water

2 green onions, cut into 2-inch pieces

¼ cup yellow miso paste

¼ cup soy sauce

2 tablespoons sake

2 tablespoons mirin

1½ teaspoons grated fresh ginger

1 teaspoon minced garlic

6 salmon fillets (about 4 ounces each)

Hot cooked rice (optional)

Thinly sliced green onions (optional)

1 Combine water, 2 green onions, miso, soy sauce, sake, mirin, ginger and garlic in Instant Pot; mix well. Add salmon to pot, skin side down.

2 Secure lid and move pressure release valve to Sealing position. Press Pressure Cook or Manual; cook at low pressure 4 minutes.

3 When cooking is complete, use quick release. Serve salmon with rice, if desired. Garnish with sliced green onions; drizzle with cooking liquid.

Tuesday Night Tacos

Makes 4 to 6 servings

1 tablespoon vegetable oil

1½ pounds boneless skinless chicken thighs

1 cup chunky salsa

Corn tortillas, warmed

½ cup shredded lettuce

1 cup pico de gallo

1 cup (4 ounces) shredded taco blend or Cheddar cheese

Lime wedges (optional)

Optional toppings: sour cream, sliced jalapeño peppers, pickled onions and/or diced avocado

1 Press Sauté; heat oil in Instant Pot. Add chicken; cook 4 to 5 minutes or until browned on both sides. Add salsa; cook 1 minute, scraping up browned bits from bottom of pot. Turn chicken to coat with salsa.

2 Secure lid and move pressure release valve to Sealing position. Press Pressure Cook or Manual; cook at high pressure 11 minutes.

3 When cooking is complete, use quick release. Use two forks or tongs to shred chicken into bite-size pieces in pot.

4 Serve chicken mixture in tortillas with lettuce, pico de gallo, cheese and lime wedges, if desired. Top as desired.

Easy Meatballs

Makes 4 servings

1 pound ground beef

1 egg, beaten

3 tablespoons Italian-seasoned dry bread crumbs

1 clove garlic, minced

1 teaspoon dried oregano

¾ teaspoon salt

¼ teaspoon black pepper

⅛ teaspoon ground red pepper

3 cups marinara or tomato-basil pasta sauce

Hot cooked spaghetti

Slivered fresh basil (optional)

Grated Parmesan cheese (optional)

1 Combine beef, egg, bread crumbs, garlic, oregano, salt, black pepper and red pepper in medium bowl; mix gently. Shape into 16 (1½-inch) meatballs.

2 Pour marinara sauce into Instant Pot. Add meatballs to sauce; turn to coat and submerge meatballs in sauce.

3 Secure lid and move pressure release valve to Sealing position. Press Pressure Cook or Manual; cook at high pressure 8 minutes.

4 When cooking is complete, use quick release. Serve meatballs and sauce over spaghetti; top with basil and cheese, if desired.

Herb Lemon Turkey Breast

Makes 4 servings

½ cup lemon juice
½ cup dry white wine
4 cloves garlic, minced
1 teaspoon salt
½ teaspoon dried parsley flakes
½ teaspoon dried tarragon
½ teaspoon dried rosemary

¼ teaspoon ground sage
¼ teaspoon black pepper
1 boneless turkey breast (about 3 pounds)
Fresh rosemary sprigs and lemon slices (optional)

1 Combine lemon juice, wine, garlic, salt, parsley flakes, tarragon, dried rosemary, sage and pepper in measuring cup or small bowl; mix well.

2 Place turkey breast in Instant Pot; pour juice mixture over turkey, turning to coat. (Turkey should be right side up for cooking.)

3 Secure lid and move pressure release valve to Sealing position. Press Pressure Cook or Manual; cook at high pressure 30 minutes.

4 When cooking is complete, use natural release for 10 minutes, then release remaining pressure. Remove turkey to cutting board; tent with foil. Let stand 10 minutes before slicing.

5 Use cooking liquid as sauce, if desired, or thicken liquid with flour (see Tip). Garnish as desired.

Tip

If desired, prepare gravy with cooking liquid after removing turkey from pot. Place ¼ cup all-purpose flour in small bowl; stir in ½ cup cooking liquid from pot until smooth. Press Sauté; add flour mixture to pot. Cook 5 minutes or until gravy thickens, stirring frequently.

Cider Pork and Onions

Makes 8 servings

- 1 tablespoon vegetable oil
- 1 bone-in pork shoulder roast (about 4 pounds)
- 4 onions, cut into ¼-inch slices (about 4 cups)
- 1 cup apple cider, divided
- 1 teaspoon salt, divided
- 4 cloves garlic, minced
- 1 teaspoon dried rosemary
- ½ teaspoon black pepper

1 Press Sauté; heat oil in Instant Pot. Add pork; cook until browned on all sides. Remove to plate. Add onions, ¼ cup cider and ½ teaspoon salt to pot; cook 8 minutes or until onions are softened, scraping up browned bits from bottom of pot. Add garlic and rosemary, cook and stir 1 minute. Return pork to pot; sprinkle with remaining ½ teaspoon salt and pepper. Pour remaining ¾ cup cider over pork.

2 Secure lid and move pressure release valve to Sealing position. Press Pressure Cook or Manual; cook at high pressure 75 minutes.

3 When cooking is complete, use natural release. Remove pork to cutting board; tent with foil.

4 Meanwhile, press Sauté; cook 10 to 15 minutes or until sauce is reduced by one third. Skim fat from sauce; season with additional salt and pepper. Cut pork; serve with sauce.

Artichoke Dijon Chicken Thighs

Makes 4 to 6 servings

1 jar (12 ounces) quartered marinated artichoke hearts, undrained

1/3 cup Dijon mustard

2 tablespoons minced garlic

1/2 teaspoon dried tarragon

1/4 teaspoon salt

2 1/2 pounds bone-in chicken thighs, skin removed

1 1/2 cups thickly sliced mushrooms

1 cup chopped onion

2 tablespoons water

1 tablespoon all-purpose flour

1/4 cup chopped fresh parsley

Hot cooked pasta (optional)

1 Drain artichokes, reserving 1/2 cup marinade. Discard remaining marinade. Combine reserved marinade, mustard, garlic, tarragon and salt in Instant Pot; mix well. Add chicken, mushrooms and onion; stir to coat.

2 Secure lid and move pressure release valve to Sealing position. Press Pressure Cook or Manual; cook at high pressure 11 minutes. When cooking is complete, use natural release for 10 minutes, then release remaining pressure.

3 Remove chicken to plate; tent with foil. Press Sauté; add artichokes to pot. Cook about 5 minutes or until sauce is reduced by half and artichokes are heated through, stirring occasionally.

4 Stir water into flour in small bowl until smooth. Add to sauce; cook and stir 1 minute or until sauce thickens. Stir in parsley. Serve chicken and sauce over pasta, if desired.

Corned Beef and Cabbage

Makes 3 to 4 servings

1 corned beef brisket (3 to 4 pounds) with seasoning packet

2 cups water

1 head cabbage (1½ pounds), cut into 6 wedges

1 package (16 ounces) baby carrots

1 Place corned beef in Instant Pot, fat side up; sprinkle with seasoning. Pour water into pot.

2 Secure lid and move pressure release valve to Sealing position. Press Pressure Cook or Manual; cook at high pressure 90 minutes.

3 When cooking is complete, use natural release for 10 minutes, then release remaining pressure. Remove beef to cutting board; tent with foil.

4 Add cabbage and carrots to pot. Secure lid and move pressure release valve to Sealing position. Press Pressure Cook or Manual; cook at high pressure 4 minutes. When cooking is complete, use quick release.

5 Slice corned beef; serve with vegetables.

Mu Shu Turkey

Makes 6 servings

1 jar (about 7 ounces) plum sauce, divided

¼ cup orange juice (juice of 1 medium orange)

¼ cup finely chopped onion

1 tablespoon minced fresh ginger

¼ teaspoon salt

¼ teaspoon ground cinnamon

1 pound boneless turkey breast or tenderloins, cut into thin strips

6 (7-inch) flour tortillas

3 cups coleslaw mix

1 Combine ⅓ cup plum sauce, orange juice, onion, ginger, salt and cinnamon in Instant Pot; mix well. Add turkey, stir to coat.

2 Secure lid and move pressure release valve to Sealing position. Press Pressure Cook or Manual; cook at high pressure 4 minutes.

3 When cooking is complete, use quick release. Press Sauté; cook 2 to 3 minutes or until sauce is reduced and thickens slightly.

4 Spread remaining jarred plum sauce over tortillas; top with turkey and coleslaw mix. Fold bottom edge of tortillas over filling; fold in sides and roll up to completely enclose filling. Serve with remaining cooking sauce for dipping.

Instant Pot
SIDES IN A SNAP

Jalapeño Cheddar Cornbread
Makes 8 servings

1 cup yellow cornmeal

¾ cup all-purpose flour

⅓ cup sugar

2 teaspoons baking powder

1 teaspoon salt

1 cup buttermilk or whole milk

2 eggs

3 tablespoons butter, melted

1 cup (4 ounces) shredded Cheddar cheese

2 jalapeño peppers, seeded and minced (about ⅓ cup)

1½ cups water

1 Spray 7-inch springform pan with nonstick cooking spray. Combine cornmeal, flour, sugar, baking powder and salt in large bowl; mix well.

2 Beat buttermilk, eggs and butter in medium bowl until blended. Add to cornmeal mixture; stir just until blended. Stir in cheese and jalapeños until blended. Spread batter evenly in prepared pan; cover with foil.

3 Pour water into Instant Pot; place rack in pot. Place pan on rack. Secure lid and move pressure release valve to Sealing position. Press Pressure Cook or Manual; cook at high pressure 30 minutes.

4 When cooking is complete, use quick release. Remove pan from pot. Uncover; cool on wire rack 5 minutes before serving.

Asparagus Risotto

Makes 4 to 6 servings

4 tablespoons (½ stick) butter, divided
1 tablespoon olive oil
1 onion, finely chopped
1½ cups uncooked arborio rice
1 teaspoon salt
¼ cup dry white wine

4 cups vegetable broth
2½ cups fresh asparagus pieces (about 1 inch)
⅔ cup frozen peas
1 cup grated Parmesan cheese
Shaved Parmesan cheese (optional)

1 Press Sauté; heat 3 tablespoons butter and oil in Instant Pot. Add onion; cook and stir 2 minutes or until softened. Add rice; cook and stir 2 minutes or until rice is translucent. Stir in salt. Add wine; cook and stir about 1 minute or until evaporated. Add broth; mix well.

2 Secure lid and move pressure release valve to Sealing position. Press Pressure Cook or Manual; cook at high pressure 5 minutes.

3 When cooking is complete, use quick release. Stir in asparagus and peas. Secure lid and move pressure release valve to Sealing position. Press Pressure Cook or Manual; cook at high pressure 1 minute.

4 When cooking is complete, use quick release. Stir in remaining 1 tablespoon butter and 1 cup cheese. Serve immediately with additional cheese, if desired.

Asparagus-Spinach Risotto

Substitute 1 cup baby spinach or chopped fresh spinach leaves for peas. Proceed as directed.

Shortcut Baked Beans

Makes 6 to 8 servings

5 slices thick-cut bacon, chopped	1 cup barbecue sauce
1 small onion, chopped	¼ cup ketchup
3½ cups water	½ teaspoon salt
1 pound dried pinto beans, rinsed and sorted	

1 Press Sauté; cook bacon in Instant Pot until crisp. Drain off all but 1 tablespoon drippings.

2 Add onion to pot; cook and stir 3 minutes or until softened. Add water and beans; cook 1 minute, scraping up browned bits from bottom of pot. Stir in barbecue sauce and ketchup; mix well.

3 Secure lid and move pressure release valve to Sealing position. Press Pressure Cook or Manual; cook at high pressure 50 minutes.

4 When cooking is complete, use natural release for 15 minutes, then release remaining pressure. Stir beans; season with ½ teaspoon salt. If there is excess liquid in pot, press Sauté and cook 3 to 5 minutes or until liquid is reduced, stirring frequently.

Parmesan Garlic Monkey Bread
Makes 6 to 8 servings

2 tablespoons butter, melted
2 tablespoons olive oil
2 cloves garlic, minced
1 teaspoon Italian seasoning
¼ teaspoon salt
1 cup grated Parmesan cheese (do not use shredded)

1 container (about 16 ounces) refrigerated jumbo biscuits (8 biscuits)
1 cup water
Pizza sauce or marinara sauce (optional)

1 Spray 6-cup bundt pan with nonstick cooking spray. Combine butter, oil, garlic, Italian seasoning and salt in medium bowl; mix well. Place cheese in shallow dish.

2 Separate biscuits; cut each biscuit into quarters. Dip each biscuit piece in butter mixture; roll in cheese to coat. Layer biscuit pieces in prepared pan; cover with foil.

3 Pour water into Instant Pot; place rack in pot. Place pan on rack. Secure lid and move pressure release valve to Sealing position. Press Pressure Cook or Manual; cook at high pressure 25 minutes. Preheat oven to 400°F. Line small baking sheet with foil; spray with cooking spray.

4 When cooking is complete, use natural release for 10 minutes, then release remaining pressure. Remove pan from pot. Uncover; let stand 10 minutes.

5 Invert monkey bread onto prepared baking sheet. Bake about 10 minutes or until top is golden brown. Serve with pizza sauce for dipping, if desired.

Spanish Rice

Makes 6 to 8 servings

1 tablespoon olive oil

1 small onion, chopped

2 cloves garlic, minced

2 cups uncooked brown rice, rinsed well and drained

1 can (about 14 ounces) diced tomatoes with green chiles

1 cup plus 2 tablespoons chicken broth or water

1 teaspoon salt

1 Press Sauté; heat oil in Instant Pot. Add onion and garlic; cook and stir 2 minutes. Add rice; cook and stir 2 minutes. Stir in tomatoes, broth and salt; mix well.

2 Secure lid and move pressure release valve to Sealing position. Press Pressure Cook or Manual; cook at high pressure 24 minutes.

3 When cooking is complete, use natural release for 10 minutes, then release remaining pressure. Fluff rice with fork.

Barley with Currants and Pine Nuts

Makes 4 to 6 servings

2 tablespoons butter

1 onion, finely chopped

2 cups vegetable broth

1 cup uncooked pearl barley

½ cup currants

½ teaspoon salt

¼ teaspoon black pepper

2 ounces (about ½ cup) pine nuts, toasted*

*To toast pine nuts, cook in small skillet over medium heat 3 minutes or until lightly browned, stirring frequently.

1 Press Sauté; melt butter in Instant Pot. Add onion; cook and stir 5 minutes or until tender. Stir in broth, barley, currants, salt and pepper; mix well.

2 Secure lid and move pressure release valve to Sealing position. Press Pressure Cook or Manual; cook at high pressure 18 minutes.

3 When cooking is complete, use natural release for 10 minutes, then release remaining pressure.

4 Stir in pine nuts. Serve warm or at room temperature.

Cheesy Polenta

Makes 6 servings

5 cups vegetable or chicken broth	¼ cup (½ stick) butter, cubed, plus additional for serving
½ teaspoon salt	Fried sage leaves (optional)
1½ cups uncooked instant polenta	
½ cup grated Parmesan cheese	

1 Combine broth and salt in Instant Pot; slowly whisk in polenta until blended.

2 Secure lid and move pressure release valve to Sealing position. Press Pressure Cook or Manual; cook at high pressure 5 minutes.

3 When cooking is complete, use natural release for 5 minutes, then release remaining pressure.

4 Whisk in cheese and ¼ cup butter until well blended. (Polenta may appear separated immediately after cooking but will come together when stirred.) Serve with additional butter; garnish with sage.

Tip

Spread any leftover polenta in a baking dish and refrigerate until cold. Cut the cold polenta into sticks or slices, brush with olive oil and pan-fry or grill until lightly browned.

Farro Risotto with Mushrooms and Spinach

Makes 4 servings

2 tablespoons olive oil, divided

1 onion, chopped

12 ounces cremini mushrooms, trimmed and quartered

1 teaspoon salt

¼ teaspoon black pepper

2 cloves garlic, minced

1 cup uncooked pearled farro

1 sprig fresh thyme

1½ cups vegetable broth

1 package (5 to 6 ounces) baby spinach

½ cup grated Parmesan cheese

1 Press Sauté; heat 1 tablespoon oil in Instant Pot. Add onion; cook and stir 5 minutes or until translucent. Add remaining 1 tablespoon oil, mushrooms, salt and pepper; cook about 8 minutes or until mushrooms have released their liquid and are browned, stirring occasionally. Add garlic; cook and stir 1 minute. Add farro and thyme; cook and stir 1 minute. Stir in broth; mix well.

2 Secure lid and move pressure release valve to Sealing position. Press Pressure Cook or Manual; cook at high pressure 10 minutes.

3 When cooking is complete, use natural release for 10 minutes, then release remaining pressure. Remove and discard thyme sprig.

4 Add spinach and cheese; stir until spinach is wilted.

Bulgur Pilaf with Caramelized Onions and Kale

Makes 4 servings

1 tablespoon olive oil

1 medium onion, cut into thin wedges

1 clove garlic, minced

2 cups chopped kale

2¾ cups vegetable or chicken broth

1 cup medium grain bulgur

1 teaspoon salt

¼ teaspoon black pepper

1 Press Sauté; heat oil in Instant Pot. Add onion; cook about 10 minutes or until golden brown, stirring frequently. Add garlic; cook and stir 1 minute. Add kale; cook and stir about 1 minute or until wilted. Stir in broth, bulgur, salt and pepper; mix well.

2 Secure lid and move pressure release valve to Sealing position. Press Pressure Cook or Manual; cook at high pressure 8 minutes.

3 When cooking is complete, use natural release for 5 minutes, then release remaining pressure.

Winter Squash Risotto

Makes 4 to 6 servings

2 tablespoons butter	¼ teaspoon black pepper
1 tablespoon olive oil	¼ cup dry white wine
1 large shallot or small onion, finely chopped	4 cups vegetable or chicken broth
1½ cups uncooked arborio rice	2 cups cubed butternut squash (½-inch pieces)
1 teaspoon salt	½ cup grated Parmesan or Romano cheese, plus additional for garnish
½ teaspoon dried thyme	

1 Press Sauté; heat butter and oil in Instant Pot. Add shallot; cook and stir 2 minutes or until softened. Add rice; cook and stir 4 minutes or until rice is translucent. Stir in salt, thyme and pepper. Add wine; cook and stir about 1 minute or until evaporated. Add broth and squash; mix well.

2 Secure lid and move pressure release valve to Sealing position. Press Pressure Cook or Manual; cook at high pressure 6 minutes.

3 When cooking is complete, use quick release.

4 Press Sauté; adjust heat to low. Cook about 3 minutes or until risotto reaches desired consistency, stirring constantly. Stir in ½ cup cheese. Serve immediately with additional cheese.

Mexican Corn Bread Pudding

Makes 8 servings

1 can (14¾ ounces) cream-style corn
¾ cup yellow cornmeal
2 eggs
1 can (4 ounces) diced mild
   green chiles
2 tablespoons vegetable oil

2 tablespoons sugar
2 teaspoons baking powder
¾ teaspoon salt
1¼ cups water
½ cup (2 ounces) shredded
   Cheddar cheese

1 Spray 6- to 7-inch (1½-quart) soufflé dish or round baking dish with nonstick cooking spray.

2 Combine corn, cornmeal, eggs, chiles, oil, sugar, baking powder and salt in medium bowl; mix well. Pour into prepared soufflé dish; cover with foil.

3 Pour water into Instant Pot; place rack in pot. Place soufflé dish on rack.

4 Secure lid and move pressure release valve to Sealing position. Press Pressure Cook or Manual; cook at high pressure 25 minutes.

5 When cooking is complete, use natural release for 10 minutes, then release remaining pressure. Remove soufflé dish from pot. Uncover; sprinkle with cheese. Tent with foil; let stand 5 minutes or until cheese is melted.

Greek Rice

Makes 6 to 8 servings

2 tablespoons butter

1¾ cups uncooked long grain rice, rinsed well and drained

1¾ cups vegetable or chicken broth

1 teaspoon Greek seasoning

1 teaspoon dried oregano

¼ teaspoon salt

1 cup pitted kalamata olives, drained and chopped

¾ cup chopped roasted red peppers

Crumbled feta cheese (optional)

Chopped fresh Italian parsley (optional)

1 Press Sauté; melt butter in Instant Pot. Add rice; cook 5 to 6 minutes or until golden brown, stirring occasionally. Add broth, Greek seasoning, oregano and salt; mix well.

2 Secure lid and move pressure release valve to Sealing position. Press Pressure Cook or Manual; cook at high pressure 4 minutes.

3 When cooking is complete, use natural release for 10 minutes, then release remaining pressure.

4 Stir in olives and roasted peppers; garnish with cheese and parsley.

Instant Pot
QUICK-COOKING VEGETABLES

Garlic Parmesan Spaghetti Squash

Makes 2 servings

1 medium spaghetti squash (2 to 2½ pounds)	¼ teaspoon salt
1 cup water	¼ teaspoon red pepper flakes
2 tablespoons extra virgin olive oil	⅛ teaspoon black pepper
1 clove garlic, minced	½ cup shredded Parmesan cheese
	⅓ cup chopped fresh parsley

1 Cut squash in half; remove and discard seeds. Pour water into Instant Pot; place rack in pot. Place squash halves on rack, cut sides up.

2 Secure lid and move pressure release valve to Sealing position. Press Pressure Cook or Manual; cook at high pressure 7 minutes.

3 When cooking is complete, use quick release. Remove squash to plate; let stand until cool enough to handle. Use fork to shred squash into long strands, reserving shells for serving, if desired.

4 Pour out cooking water and dry pot with paper towel. Press Sauté; adjust heat to low. Add oil, garlic, salt, red pepper flakes and black pepper to pot; cook and stir 2 to 3 minutes or until garlic begins to turn golden. Turn off heat. Add squash, cheese and parsley; cook and stir gently just until blended. Serve immediately.

Mashed Potatoes with Bacon and Cabbage

Makes 6 to 8 servings

4 slices bacon, chopped

3 pounds russet potatoes, peeled and cut into 1-inch pieces

2 medium leeks, halved lengthwise and thinly sliced

½ cup water

1¼ teaspoons salt

¼ teaspoon black pepper

1 cup milk, divided

2 tablespoons butter, cut into small pieces

½ small head savoy cabbage (about 1 pound), cored and thinly sliced (about 4 cups)

1 Press Sauté; cook bacon in Instant Pot until crisp. Remove to paper towel-lined plate. Add potatoes, leeks, water, salt and pepper to pot; mix well.

2 Secure lid and move pressure release valve to Sealing position. Press Pressure Cook or Manual; cook at high pressure 5 minutes.

3 When cooking is complete, use quick release.

4 Press Sauté; add ½ cup milk and butter to pot. Cook and stir 1 minute, mashing potatoes with potato masher or fork until still slightly chunky. Add remaining ½ cup milk and cabbage; cook and stir 2 to 3 minutes or until cabbage is wilted. Stir in bacon.

Beet and Arugula Salad

Makes 6 servings

1 cup water
8 medium beets (5 to 6 ounces each)
⅓ cup red wine vinegar
¾ teaspoon salt

½ teaspoon black pepper
3 tablespoons extra virgin olive oil
1 package (5 ounces) baby arugula
1 package (4 ounces) goat cheese with garlic and herbs, crumbled

1 Pour water into Instant Pot; place rack in pot. Arrange beets on rack (or use steamer basket to hold beets). Secure lid and move pressure release valve to Sealing position. Press Pressure Cook or Manual; cook at high pressure 20 minutes.

2 When cooking is complete, use natural release for 10 minutes, then release remaining pressure. Set beets aside until cool enough to handle.

3 Meanwhile, whisk vinegar, salt and pepper in large bowl. Slowly add oil in thin, steady stream, whisking until well blended. Remove 3 tablespoons dressing to medium bowl.

4 Peel beets and cut into wedges. Add warm beets to large bowl; toss to coat with dressing. Add arugula to medium bowl; toss gently to coat with dressing. Place arugula on platter or plates, top with beets and cheese.

Parmesan Potato Wedges

Makes 4 to 6 servings

2 pounds unpeeled red potatoes (about 6 medium), cut into ½-inch wedges

½ cup water

¼ cup finely chopped onion

2 tablespoons butter, cut into small pieces

1¼ teaspoons salt

1 teaspoon dried oregano

¼ teaspoon black pepper

¼ cup grated Parmesan cheese

1 Combine potatoes, water, onion, butter, salt, oregano and pepper in Instant Pot; mix well.

2 Secure lid and move pressure release valve to Sealing position. Press Pressure Cook or Manual; cook at high pressure 3 minutes.

3 When cooking is complete, use quick release. Transfer potatoes to serving platter; sprinkle with cheese.

Butternut Squash with Apples and Walnuts

Makes 4 servings

1 tablespoon butter

1 medium Granny Smith apple, peeled and cut into ½-inch pieces

3 cups cubed peeled butternut squash (¾-inch cubes)

½ cup water

3 tablespoons dried cranberries

2 teaspoons packed brown sugar

½ teaspoon salt

¼ teaspoon ground cinnamon

⅛ teaspoon black pepper

2 tablespoons chopped walnuts

1 Press Sauté; melt butter in Instant Pot. Add apple; cook about 5 minutes or until tender, stirring occasionally. Remove to plate; set aside. Add squash, water, cranberries, brown sugar, salt, cinnamon and pepper to pot; stir until sugar is dissolved.

2 Secure lid and move pressure release valve to Sealing position. Press Pressure Cook or Manual; cook at high pressure 1 minute.

3 When cooking is complete, use quick release.

4 Press Sauté; add cooked apple to pot. Cook 2 minutes or until heated through, stirring occasionally. Gently stir in walnuts.

Chunky Ranch Potatoes

Makes 8 servings

3 pounds unpeeled red potatoes, quartered

½ cup water

1 teaspoon salt

½ cup ranch dressing

½ cup grated Parmesan cheese

¼ cup minced fresh chives

1 Combine potatoes, water and salt in Instant Pot; mix well.

2 Secure lid and move pressure release valve to Sealing position. Press Pressure Cook or Manual; cook at high pressure 5 minutes.

3 When cooking is complete, use quick release.

4 Add ranch dressing, cheese and chives to pot; stir gently to coat, breaking potatoes into chunks.

Quicker Collard Greens

Makes 4 to 6 servings

4 slices thick-cut bacon, cut into ½-inch pieces

1 pound collard greens, stems trimmed, roughly chopped

½ cup water or chicken broth

1 tablespoon cider vinegar

1 tablespoon packed brown sugar

¼ teaspoon salt

¼ teaspoon black pepper

¼ teaspoon red pepper flakes

1 Press Sauté; cook bacon in Instant Pot until crisp. Add half of greens; cook 1 minute or until greens begin to wilt, scraping up browned bits from bottom of pot. Add remaining greens; cook and stir 1 minute. Stir in water, vinegar, brown sugar, salt, black pepper and red pepper flakes; mix well.

2 Secure lid and move pressure release valve to Sealing position. Press Pressure Cook or Manual; cook at high pressure 20 minutes.

3 When cooking is complete, use quick release. Stir greens; serve warm.

Mashed Sweet Potatoes and Parsnips

Makes 6 servings

2 large sweet potatoes (about 1½ pounds), peeled and cut into 1-inch pieces

2 medium parsnips (about 12 ounces), peeled and cut into ½-inch slices

½ cup water

1 teaspoon salt

¼ cup evaporated milk

2 tablespoons butter

⅛ teaspoon ground nutmeg

¼ cup chopped fresh chives or green onions

1 Combine sweet potatoes, parsnips, water and salt in Instant Pot. Secure lid and move pressure release valve to Sealing position. Press Pressure Cook or Manual; cook at high pressure 10 minutes.

2 When cooking is complete, use quick release.

3 Add milk, butter and nutmeg to pot; mash with potato masher until smooth. Stir in chives.

Balsamic Green Beans with Almonds

Makes 4 servings

1 cup water
1 pound fresh green beans, trimmed
1 tablespoon extra virgin olive oil
2 teaspoons balsamic vinegar
½ teaspoon salt

¼ teaspoon black pepper
2 tablespoons sliced almonds, toasted*

To toast almonds, cook in small skillet over medium heat 1 to 2 minutes or until lightly browned, stirring frequently.

1 Pour water into Instant Pot; place rack in pot. Place beans on rack. (Arrange beans perpendicular to rack to prevent beans from falling through.)

2 Secure lid and move pressure release valve to Sealing position. Press Pressure Cook or Manual; cook at high pressure 2 minutes.

3 When cooking is complete, use quick release. Remove rack from pot; place beans in large bowl.

4 Add oil, vinegar, salt and pepper; toss to coat. Sprinkle with almonds just before serving.

Cauliflower and Potato Masala

Makes 6 servings

1 tablespoon olive or vegetable oil

2 teaspoons minced garlic

1 teaspoon minced fresh ginger

1 teaspoon salt

1 teaspoon cumin seeds *or*
    ½ teaspoon ground cumin

1 teaspoon ground coriander

1 teaspoon garam masala

1 can (about 14 ounces)
    diced tomatoes

1 head cauliflower (about
    1¼ pounds), broken into florets

1 pound red potatoes (2 large),
    peeled and cut into ½-inch
    wedges

2 tablespoons chopped fresh
    cilantro

1 Press Sauté; heat oil in Instant Pot. Add garlic, ginger, salt, cumin, coriander and garam masala; cook and stir about 30 seconds or until fragrant. Add tomatoes; cook and stir 1 minute. Add cauliflower and potatoes; mix well.

2 Secure lid and move pressure release valve to Sealing position. Press Pressure Cook or Manual; cook at high pressure 2 minutes.

3 When cooking is complete, use quick release. Sprinkle with cilantro.

Instant Pot
SIMPLE SWEETS

Big Chocolate Chip Cookie
Makes 6 to 8 servings

1 cup plus 2 tablespoons all-purpose flour

½ teaspoon baking soda

½ teaspoon salt

¼ cup (½ stick) butter, softened

½ cup packed brown sugar

2 tablespoons granulated sugar

1 egg

½ teaspoon vanilla

1 cup semisweet chocolate chunks or chips

1 cup water

1 Spray 7-inch metal cake pan with nonstick cooking spray. Combine flour, baking soda and salt in small bowl; mix well.

2 Beat butter, brown sugar and granulated sugar in medium bowl with electric mixer at medium speed until light and creamy. Add egg and vanilla; beat until well blended. Add flour mixture; beat just until blended. Stir in chocolate chunks. Spread batter in prepared pan. Cover pan with paper towel (to absorb moisture), making sure paper towel does not touch batter. Cover pan with foil over paper towel.

3 Pour water into Instant Pot; place rack in pot. Place pan on rack. Secure lid and move pressure release valve to Sealing position. Press Pressure Cook or Manual; cook at high pressure 35 minutes.

4 When cooking is complete, use natural release for 10 minutes, then release remaining pressure. Remove pan from pot. Uncover; cool on wire rack 15 minutes. Invert cookie onto plate; invert again onto serving plate. Serve warm or at room temperature.

Pumpkin Custard

Makes 6 servings

3 eggs

1 can (15 ounces) pure pumpkin

1 can (14 ounces) sweetened
   condensed milk

1 teaspoon ground cinnamon,
   plus additional for garnish

1 teaspoon finely chopped candied
   ginger *or* ½ teaspoon ground
   ginger

¼ teaspoon ground cloves

⅛ teaspoon salt

1 cup water

   Whipped cream (optional)

1 Beat eggs in medium bowl. Add pumpkin, sweetened condensed milk, 1 teaspoon cinnamon, ginger, cloves and salt; beat until well blended and smooth. Pour into six 6-ounce ramekins or custard cups. Cover each ramekin tightly with foil.

2 Pour water into Instant Pot; place rack in pot. Arrange ramekins on rack, stacking as necessary.

3 Secure lid and move pressure release valve to Sealing position. Press Pressure Cook or Manual; cook at high pressure 8 minutes.

4 When cooking is complete, use natural release. Remove ramekins from pot. Uncover; cool to room temperature. Refrigerate until chilled. Top with whipped cream and additional cinnamon, if desired.

Spiced Chocolate Bread Pudding

Makes 6 to 8 servings

1½ cups whipping cream

4 ounces unsweetened chocolate, coarsely chopped

2 eggs

½ cup sugar

1 teaspoon vanilla

¾ teaspoon ground cinnamon, plus additional for garnish

½ teaspoon ground allspice

⅛ teaspoon salt

3 cups cubed Hawaiian-style sweet bread, challah or brioche bread (½-inch cubes)

½ cup currants

1¼ cups water

Whipped cream (optional)

1 Spray 6- to 7-inch (1½-quart) soufflé dish or round baking dish with nonstick cooking spray. Heat cream to a simmer in medium saucepan over medium heat. Remove from heat. Add chocolate; stir until melted and smooth.

2 Beat eggs in large bowl. Add sugar, vanilla, ¾ teaspoon cinnamon, allspice and salt; mix well. Add chocolate mixture; stir until well blended. Add bread cubes and currants; stir gently to coat. Pour into prepared soufflé dish; cover with foil.

3 Pour water into Instant Pot; place rack in pot. Place soufflé dish on rack.

4 Secure lid and move pressure release valve to Sealing position. Press Pressure Cook or Manual; cook at high pressure 35 minutes.

5 When cooking is complete, use natural release for 10 minutes, then release remaining pressure. Remove soufflé dish from pot. Uncover; cool 15 minutes. Serve warm or at room temperature. Top with whipped cream and additional cinnamon, if desired.

Peanut Butter Pudding

Makes 6 servings

2 cups milk
2 eggs
⅓ cup creamy peanut butter
¼ cup packed brown sugar

¼ teaspoon vanilla
1 cup water
Shaved chocolate or shredded coconut (optional)

1 Spray six 3-ounce ramekins or custard cups with nonstick cooking spray. Combine milk, eggs, peanut butter, brown sugar and vanilla in blender; blend at high speed 1 minute. Pour into prepared ramekins. Cover each ramekin tightly with foil.

2 Pour water into Instant Pot; place rack in pot. Arrange ramekins on rack, stacking as necessary.

3 Secure lid and move pressure release valve to Sealing position. Press Pressure Cook or Manual; cook at high pressure 8 minutes.

4 When cooking is complete, use natural release for 10 minutes, then release remaining pressure. Remove ramekins from pot. Uncover; cool to room temperature. Refrigerate until chilled. Garnish with shaved chocolate.

Fudgy Double Chocolate Brownies

Makes 8 servings

½ cup (1 stick) butter
¾ cup unsweetened cocoa powder
1 cup sugar
2 eggs
⅔ cup all-purpose flour

½ teaspoon salt
½ cup semisweet chocolate chunks
   or chips
1½ cups water
Vanilla ice cream (optional)

1 Spray 7-inch metal cake pan with nonstick cooking spray. Line bottom of pan with parchment paper; spray with cooking spray. Place butter in medium microwavable bowl; microwave until melted. Stir in cocoa until well blended.

2 Beat sugar and eggs in large bowl until well blended. Add cocoa mixture; stir until smooth. Add flour and salt; stir until well blended. Stir in chocolate chunks. Spread batter in prepared pan; smooth top. Cover pan with paper towel (to absorb moisture), making sure paper towel does not touch batter. Cover pan with foil over paper towel.

3 Pour water into Instant Pot; place rack in pot. Place pan on rack. Secure lid and move pressure release valve to Sealing position. Press Pressure Cook or Manual; cook at high pressure 25 minutes.

4 When cooking is complete, use natural release for 10 minutes, then release remaining pressure. Remove pan from pot. Uncover; cool on wire rack at least 10 minutes before serving. Invert brownie onto plate; remove parchment paper. Invert again onto serving plate. Serve warm or at room temperature with ice cream, if desired.

Southern Sweet Potato Custard

Makes 4 servings

1 can (16 ounces) cut sweet potatoes, drained

1 can (12 ounces) evaporated milk, divided

½ cup packed brown sugar

2 eggs

1 teaspoon ground cinnamon

½ teaspoon ground ginger

¼ teaspoon salt

1¼ cups water

Whipped cream (optional)

Ground nutmeg (optional)

1 Combine sweet potatoes and ¼ cup evaporated milk in food processor or blender; process until smooth. Add remaining evaporated milk, brown sugar, eggs, cinnamon, ginger and salt; process until well blended. Pour into 6- to 7-inch (1½-quart) soufflé dish or round baking dish; cover with foil.

2 Pour water into Instant Pot; place rack in pot. Place soufflé dish on rack.

3 Secure lid and move pressure release valve to Sealing position. Press Pressure Cook or Manual; cook at high pressure 40 minutes.

4 When cooking is complete, use natural release for 10 minutes, then release remaining pressure. Remove soufflé dish from pot. Uncover; cool 30 minutes. Garnish with whipped cream and nutmeg.

Rich Chocolate Pudding

Makes 6 servings

1½ cups whipping cream

4 ounces bittersweet chocolate, chopped

4 egg yolks

⅓ cup packed brown sugar

1 tablespoon unsweetened cocoa powder

1 teaspoon vanilla

¼ teaspoon salt

1¼ cups water

1 Heat cream to a simmer in medium saucepan over medium heat. Remove from heat. Add chocolate; stir until chocolate is melted and mixture is smooth.

2 Beat egg yolks, brown sugar, cocoa, vanilla and salt in large bowl until well blended. Gradually add warm chocolate mixture, stirring constantly until blended. Strain into 6- to 7-inch (1½-quart) soufflé dish or round baking dish; cover with foil.

3 Pour water into Instant Pot; place rack in pot. Place soufflé dish on rack.

4 Secure lid and move pressure release valve to Sealing position. Press Pressure Cook or Manual; cook at low pressure 22 minutes.

5 When cooking is complete, use natural release for 5 minutes, then release remaining pressure. Remove soufflé dish from pot. Uncover; cool to room temperature. Cover and refrigerate at least 3 hours or up to 2 days.

Superfast Applesauce

Makes 4 cups

2 pounds (about 4 medium) sweet apples (such as Fuji, Gala or Honeycrisp), peeled and cut into 1-inch pieces

2 pounds (about 4 medium) Granny Smith apples, peeled and cut into 1-inch pieces

⅓ cup water

2 to 4 tablespoons packed brown sugar, divided

1 tablespoon lemon juice

1 teaspoon ground cinnamon

⅛ teaspoon salt

⅛ teaspoon ground nutmeg

⅛ teaspoon ground cloves

1 Combine apples, water, 2 tablespoons brown sugar, lemon juice, cinnamon, salt, nutmeg and cloves in Instant Pot; mix well.

2 Secure lid and move pressure release valve to Sealing position. Press Pressure Cook or Manual; cook at high pressure 4 minutes.

3 When cooking is complete, use quick release.

4 Stir applesauce; taste for seasoning and add remaining 2 tablespoons brown sugar, if desired. If there is excess liquid in pot, press Sauté and cook 2 to 3 minutes or until liquid evaporates. Cool completely before serving.

Pumpkin Bread Pudding

Makes 4 servings

1 cup whole milk
2 eggs
½ cup canned pumpkin
⅓ cup packed brown sugar
1 tablespoon butter, melted
1½ teaspoons ground cinnamon
1 teaspoon vanilla

¼ teaspoon salt
¼ teaspoon ground nutmeg
8 slices cinnamon raisin bread, torn into small pieces (about 4 cups)
1¼ cups water
Prepared caramel sauce or ice cream topping (optional)

1 Spray 6- to 7-inch (1½-quart) soufflé dish or round baking dish with nonstick cooking spray. Beat milk, eggs, pumpkin, brown sugar, butter, cinnamon, vanilla, salt and nutmeg in large bowl until well blended. Add bread cubes; stir gently to coat. Pour into prepared soufflé dish; cover with foil.

2 Pour water into Instant Pot; place rack in pot. Place soufflé dish on rack.

3 Secure lid and move pressure release valve to Sealing position. Press Pressure Cook or Manual; cook at high pressure 40 minutes.

4 When cooking is complete, use natural release for 10 minutes, then release remaining pressure. Remove soufflé dish from pot. Uncover; cool 15 minutes. Serve warm with caramel sauce, if desired.

Instant Pot

PRESSURE COOKING TIMES

Meat

Meat	MINUTES UNDER PRESSURE	PRESSURE	RELEASE
Beef, Bone-in Short Ribs	35 to 45	High	Natural
Beef, Brisket	60 to 75	High	Natural
Beef, Ground	8	High	Natural
Beef, Roast (round, rump or shoulder)	60 to 70	High	Natural
Beef, Stew Meat	20 to 25	High	Natural or Quick
Lamb, Chops	5 to 10	High	Quick
Lamb, Leg or Shanks	35 to 40	High	Natural
Lamb, Stew Meat	12 to 15	High	Quick
Pork, Baby Back Ribs	25 to 30	High	Natural
Pork, Chops	7 to 10	High	Quick
Pork, Ground	5	High	Quick
Pork, Loin	15 to 25	High	Natural
Pork, Shoulder or Butt	45 to 60	High	Natural
Pork, Stew Meat	15 to 20	High	Quick

Poultry

Poultry	MINUTES UNDER PRESSURE	PRESSURE	RELEASE
Chicken Breasts, Bone-in	7 to 10	High	Quick
Chicken Breasts, Boneless	5 to 8	High	Quick
Chicken Thigh, Bone-in	10 to 14	High	Natural
Chicken Thigh, Boneless	8 to 10	High	Natural
Chicken Wings	10 to 12	High	Quick

Chicken, Whole	22 to 26	High	Natural
Eggs, Hard-Cooked (3 to 12)	9	Low	Quick
Turkey Breast, Bone-in	25 to 30	High	Natural
Turkey Breast, Boneless	15 to 20	High	Natural
Turkey Legs	35 to 40	High	Natural
Turkey, Ground	8 to 10	High	Quick

Seafood

Seafood	MINUTES UNDER PRESSURE	PRESSURE	RELEASE
Cod	2 to 3	Low	Quick
Crab	2 to 3	Low	Quick
Halibut	6	Low	Quick
Mussels	1 to 2	Low	Quick
Salmon	4 to 5	Low	Quick
Scallops	1	Low	Quick
Shrimp	2 to 3	Low	Quick
Swordfish	4 to 5	Low	Quick
Tilapia	3	Low	Quick

Dried Beans and Legumes

Dried Beans and Legumes	UNSOAKED	SOAKED	PRESSURE	RELEASE
Black Beans	22 to 25	8 to 10	High	Natural
Black-Eyed Peas	9 to 11	3 to 5	High	Natural
Cannellini Beans	30 to 35	8 to 10	High	Natural
Chickpeas	35 to 40	18 to 22	High	Natural
Great Northern Beans	25 to 30	7 to 10	High	Natural

Instant Pot

Kidney Beans	20 to 25	8 to 12	High	Natural
Lentils, Brown or Green	10 to 12	n/a	High	Natural
Lentils, Red or Yellow Split	1	n/a	High	Natural
Navy Beans	20 to 25	7 to 8	High	Natural
Pinto Beans	22 to 25	8 to 10	High	Natural
Split Peas	8 to 10	n/a	High	Natural

Grains

Grains	LIQUID PER CUP	MINUTES UNDER PRESSURE	PRESSURE	RELEASE
Barley, Pearl	2	18 to 22	High	Natural
Barley, Whole	2½	30 to 35	High	Natural
Bulgur	3	8	High	Natural
Farro	2	10 to 12	High	Natural
Grits, Medium	4	12 to 15	High	10 minute natural
Millet	1½	1	High	Natural
Oats, Rolled	2	4 to 5	High	10 minute natural
Oats, Steel-Cut	3	10 to 13	High	10 minute natural
Quinoa	1½	1	High	10 minute natural
Polenta, Instant	3	5	High	5 minute natural
Rice, Arborio	2	6 to 7	High	Quick
Rice, Brown	1	22	High	10 minute natural
Rice, White Long Grain	1	4	High	10 minute natural

Vegetables

Vegetables	MINUTES UNDER PRESSURE	PRESSURE	RELEASE
Artichokes, Whole	9 to 12	High	Natural
Beets, Medium Whole	18 to 24	High	Quick
Brussels Sprouts, Whole	2 to 3	High	Quick

Cabbage, Sliced	3 to 5	High	Quick
Carrots, Sliced	2 to 4	High	Quick
Cauliflower, Florets	2 to 3	High	Quick
Cauliflower, Whole	3 to 5	High	Quick
Corn on the Cob	2 to 4	High	Quick
Eggplant	3 to 4	High	Quick
Fennel, Sliced	3 to 4	High	Quick
Green Beans	2 to 4	High	Quick
Kale	3	High	Quick
Leeks	3	High	Quick
Okra	3	High	Quick
Potatoes, Baby or Fingerling	6 to 10	High	Natural
Potatoes, New	7 to 9	High	Natural
Potatoes, 1-inch pieces	4 to 6	High	Quick
Potatoes, Sweet, 1-inch pieces	3	High	Quick
Potatoes, Sweet, Whole	8 to 12	High	Natural
Spinach	1	High	Quick
Squash, Acorn, Halved	7	High	Natural
Squash, Butternut, 1-inch pieces	4 to 6	High	Quick
Squash, Spaghetti, Halved	6 to 10	High	Natural
Tomatoes, cut into pieces for sauce	5	High	Natural

METRIC CONVERSION CHART

VOLUME MEASUREMENTS (dry)

1/8 teaspoon = 0.5 mL
1/4 teaspoon = 1 mL
1/2 teaspoon = 2 mL
3/4 teaspoon = 4 mL
1 teaspoon = 5 mL
1 tablespoon = 15 mL
2 tablespoons = 30 mL
1/4 cup = 60 mL
1/3 cup = 75 mL
1/2 cup = 125 mL
2/3 cup = 150 mL
3/4 cup = 175 mL
1 cup = 250 mL
2 cups = 1 pint = 500 mL
3 cups = 750 mL
4 cups = 1 quart = 1 L

VOLUME MEASUREMENTS (fluid)

1 fluid ounce (2 tablespoons) = 30 mL
4 fluid ounces (1/2 cup) = 125 mL
8 fluid ounces (1 cup) = 250 mL
12 fluid ounces (1 1/2 cups) = 375 mL
16 fluid ounces (2 cups) = 500 mL

WEIGHTS (mass)

1/2 ounce = 15 g
1 ounce = 30 g
3 ounces = 90 g
4 ounces = 120 g
8 ounces = 225 g
10 ounces = 285 g
12 ounces = 360 g
16 ounces = 1 pound = 450 g

DIMENSIONS

1/16 inch = 2 mm
1/8 inch = 3 mm
1/4 inch = 6 mm
1/2 inch = 1.5 cm
3/4 inch = 2 cm
1 inch = 2.5 cm

OVEN TEMPERATURES

250°F = 120°C
275°F = 140°C
300°F = 150°C
325°F = 160°C
350°F = 180°C
375°F = 190°C
400°F = 200°C
425°F = 220°C
450°F = 230°C

BAKING PAN SIZES

Utensil	Size in Inches/Quarts	Metric Volume	Size in Centimeters
Baking or Cake Pan (square or rectangular)	8×8×2	2 L	20×20×5
	9×9×2	2.5 L	23×23×5
	12×8×2	3 L	30×20×5
	13×9×2	3.5 L	33×23×5
Loaf Pan	8×4×3	1.5 L	20×10×7
	9×5×3	2 L	23×13×7
Round Layer Cake Pan	8×1½	1.2 L	20×4
	9×1½	1.5 L	23×4
Pie Plate	8×1¼	750 mL	20×3
	9×1¼	1 L	23×3
Baking Dish or Casserole	1 quart	1 L	—
	1½ quart	1.5 L	—
	2 quart	2 L	—